# UNMAPPING THE 21ST CENTURY

## Between Networks and the State

Nicholas Michelsen and Neville Bolt

BRISTOL
UNIVERSITY
PRESS

First published in Great Britain in 2022 by

Bristol University Press
University of Bristol
1–9 Old Park Hill
Bristol
BS2 8BB
UK
t: +44 (0)117 374 6645
e: bup-info@bristol.ac.uk

Details of international sales and distribution partners are available at bristoluniversitypress.co.uk

© Bristol University Press 2022

British Library Cataloguing in Publication Data
A catalogue record for this book is available from the British Library

ISBN 978-1-5292-2373-6 hardcover
ISBN 978-1-5292-2374-3 paperback
ISBN 978-1-5292-2375-0 ePub
ISBN 978-1-5292-2376-7 ePdf

The right of Nicholas Michelsen and Neville Bolt to be identified as authors of this work has been asserted by them in accordance with the Copyright, Designs and Patents Act 1988.

Cover design: Clifford Hayes
Front cover image: unsplash / rufat mammadov
Bristol University Press uses environmentally responsible print partners.
Printed in Great Britain by CMP, Poole

# Contents

# List of Figures

# Introduction

The 21st century has been described as an age of turbulence.[1] What might a map of this present look like? After all, a map is only ever a snapshot of a moment in time. And our historical moment—so scholars, policymakers, and journalists tell us—is born of accelerating crises. A global pandemic following soon after the near collapse of the world's economies, enduring geopolitical conflicts, and a tide of populism threaten to overwhelm the values of democracies which have lost their self-confidence to the bemusement of authoritarian states. Popular protests target everything from environmental collapse to mass migration and racial injustice. Close to home, processes in people's lives seem to fragment before reforming in unfamiliar ways; dynamic changes are sweeping the globe, bringing chaos and unpredictability[2] while frustrating hopes for predicting or crafting a shared future. This has seeded a rising pessimism about the direction of world politics.[3] It runs through our societies, affecting the way we view economic decline, ecological shifts, and violence.

Forces of change, we are told, are reconfiguring the lines on the map—those selfsame national lines that in recent centuries have defined where and how we live. As migration, pandemics, and shocks of nature take on the appearance of energy flows that circulate the globe with little or no respect for borders, a quiet yet deeply felt nostalgia for a less complex era is growing. In response, the state is flexing its muscles. Seeking to redraw those lines—only more emphatically than before. Is our future, in some sense, fated to be the past of separate nations and sharply drawn borders?

The state is projecting itself as the arbiter of how we should make sense of contemporary turmoil. Nowhere is this more apparent than in relation to COVID-19—a coronavirus which has indiscriminately struck down populations in its path. The pandemic's lack of concern for borders between nations, and vulnerabilities of young and old, is yet to be captured on our maps of the spreading virus. People and experts are more concerned with the ways our nation states have responded, for better or worse. Maps of the pandemic list fatalities and infections by nation; and it is by nation that the numbers are calculated.

So much for the global village that was once the refrain of more optimistic decades. Perhaps it's unsurprising. We are, it has been said, living in a period of remarkable 'stasis'[4] in the map of nations, in stark contrast to the previous century, during the course of which many new states were born and others vanished. This is what is expressed in the ways we visualize the viral pandemic. Static national borders define our understanding of the virus as it spreads across human populations. National lines divide and parcel up the pandemic on the page while barely interrupting its progress on the ground. However, they still manage to say something important about the maps we use to navigate this moment in our lives.

*Unmapping the 21st Century* re-evaluates the principal maps— the state and the network—that dominate thinking about the present by citizens, journalists, policymakers, and academics alike. We invite our readers to see what is at stake when these maps are used to express the common sense of our age. And we highlight how their convenience as heuristics or shortcuts blind us to the way maps create the very futures that we fear.

Maps have always held a powerful attraction for thinkers, politicians, and policymakers, not forgetting ordinary people. Even more so at times when they find themselves adrift in the uncertainties of their lives. Maps are easily confused with the territories they claim to represent. *Unmapping the 21st Century* does not suggest that the map is simply a metaphor—the window or picture is employed to frame an idea, while the lens is used to denote the constraints of perspective. Maps matter for thinking about our present, because they express archetypes of ways of seeing. Nor are maps simply practical tools for navigating obstacles and finding the shortest road from A to B. They deploy graphic logics, whether vertical or horizontal, that layer spatial diagrams onto what we see. We imagine the world through these ideal maps, which our mind's eye superimposes onto the world around us; and then we rely on those maps to take action—to work out where to go and how to get there.

*Unmapping the 21st Century* exposes the workings of our most cherished maps of our place in time, centred on twin ideals—the map of the horizontally distributed network and the map of the hierarchically structured state—which proffer contradictory explanations of the order of things. The world is made, we suggest, not distinct from these mappings of it, but through the ways their logics intersect and consequently shape what we see. Only by recognizing this constant intersection between maps can we create clearer pathways to thought and action.

COVID-19 has injected an urgency into reflections on how climatic processes are a source of the turbulence shaping our world. The dominant maps of this pandemic reveal in stark visuals the defining paradox of the 21st century. Faced by a force of nature with no ties to any particular place—a force that attacks the universal human body—populations are caught up in a process that is flat and global. It moves above and beyond the borders of national communities; it cares for neither. Transported by aircraft, by ship, and on foot, viruses live in the networks that the globalizing 20th century created. To extend its reach and find new hosts, the pandemic relies on a dense web of international linkages designed for trade and tourism. Which surely means that managing the disease requires mobilizing those selfsame networks and the global institutions that have arisen around them.

Yet the territorial state remains our most reliable tool by which to understand the virus and take action. National responses have been diverse, as every map of the disease shows. The consequences of wealth, national geography, urbanization, health infrastructure, and socialization within each state and between all states seem to presage a creeping trend towards renationalizing a global order that marked preceding decades. Simultaneously, at the level of our digital life, an explosion of conspiracy theories and distrust through online media—not just around whether people should vaccinate or not—has been nudged by state forces, creating a mirror pandemic at the level of scientific information, deliberate disinformation, and unwitting misinformation. The map of state intermingles with global perceptions and misperceptions before folding back on itself to create a sense of inevitable transition from the newer flat world back to the older map of nations.

What is at stake is not simply seeing states as a complex set of institutions, each with its own history. Rather, it is the state as a map of the present: a governing ideal organized by a logic which is hierarchical and vertically integrated. To see the state as a map is to see it not simply as a contingent historical formation, but as a diagram for how things work. As subsequent chapters reveal, that ideal map—a vertical diagram or organogram of the state—infiltrates all our understandings and attempts to respond to processes which purport to be free or distinct from the state: from urbanization to regionalization to terrorism, migration, and climate change, as well as pandemics. And indeed the feature of hierarchy is at work in all of these.

Simply exposing the limits of the map of state as a representational tool does not offer a way forward. It often masks an equally problematic reliance on another ideal map. The state is not the only diagram for governing today or for assembling power and influence in world politics. Increasingly, it finds itself in competition with the horizontal network as the map of 21st-century life. The state map, governed by a logic of vertical integration to ease command and control, is simply one shortcut for mapping contemporary turbulence. Appealing and simple, it promises the organizational capacity to manage the uncertainties that complicate our lives. Yet complex networks have become the rival diagram of this digital age, offering to make alternative sense of the erratic, discontinuous, and random disasters that strike us.

For all the paeans to our networked age, there is little at the fundamental or grassroots level that is truly new here. Digital networks that proliferated in the consumer-led explosion of information and communications technologies come to ground in the all too human networks of family and friends. These spread across continents and have always been at the heart of human development. They enable what technologists call a multiplier effect for dynamic flows of information which, due to the logic of digital technologies, connect populations and can lead to unpredictable and explosive outcomes. That said, the novelty of today's complexity cannot be taken for granted: what is revealed by a fresh look at today's network map is an understanding of our place in history and, significantly, how people read the present in a long-term trajectory which has been defined by hierarchies but is now threatened by their breakdown and replacement by complex networks.

In this imaginary, the old world functioned because everything was ordered vertically from above, both within and beyond states. In the new world, complex networks would rule—horizontally and in unexpected ways. This vision was in part a reflection on the end of the Cold War.[5] Commentators who wrote about networks attempted to remap the world with an eye to 'connectivity ... linkage, marginality, liminality, and transgression'—in other words, attaching a revised vocabulary to the interstate system as the twin poles of the United States and the USSR that characterized the Cold War gave way to multipolarity in the new millennium.[6] The new roadmap to the 21st century assumed that borders of nation states would continue to erode only for complex networks to emerge and underpin a new global order.[7] This was to be an organic process—as the world became more complex, hierarchies would dissolve and, with them, so too would the state.

Criss-crossed by movements of capital, migrants, and refugees, and intersected by flows of protests, emotions, and ideas, the turn of the new century would come to see the sovereign lines of nation states as fragile constructs.[8] From the 'borderlands' to the centre of the international system, the lines of that system appeared to become increasingly permeable.[9] Complex networks spilled across borders in global politics, introducing the near to the far, the intimate to the unknown. Map-makers of this new present—academics, journalists, and, perhaps most perceptively, novelists—hoped to capture the uncertainties of a networked world, reading them as the inevitable downsides of progress.[10] Governments, meanwhile, would develop tools for network mapping in the hope of securing themselves scientifically from the impending risks of 21st-century life.[11] The network map was guide and call to action.

But those new networks proved to be not so new after all.[12] Evangelists, colonizers, secret societies, mercenaries, merchants, capitalists, immigrants, and emigrants have always bound the world together, linking big and small, powerful and weak states. The complexities of our age mirror, through a distorted looking glass, those of the century before, and others before that. Technologies like the telegram, telephone, steamship, automobile, and aircraft, not to mention the command structures of the skyscraper, factory conveyor belt, and typing pool, wreaked their own disruptive novelty on the world of late 19th- and early 20th-century nation states. A constant tension with flatter organization—structurelessness, networking, and non-linear interaction—had nevertheless always been there. It simply became shrouded by the modernizing drive. The Victorian butterfly collector's ambition to capture and order, to catalogue and label, was only the microcosm of a bigger enterprise: the bureaucratizing of a command-and-control hierarchy constructed on principles of scientific management and public administration. Put simply, our sense of the complexity of the new was only ever the artefact of our faulty maps—the selfsame maps that spoke of imposing fixed architectures on dynamic movement.

US and Soviet geopolitical bipolarity during the Cold War would soon give way to the twin hegemons of American military unipolarity and American and Chinese economic multipolarity. By replacing one hierarchical matrix with another, they froze the way people understood world politics.[13] Meanwhile, all kinds of emerging dynamics lay hidden, bubbling beneath the surface of the great power contest—not least the ecological catastrophe now unfolding and the 'vapour' of Islamist extremism that would ignite the war on terror. These became visible only as symptoms of a 'new complexity' when the Soviet Union dissolved and as unipolarity elided into multipolarity. A tenuous politics emerged from the 2008 global financial crisis, shaping a temporary solidity that appeared more like a shaky status quo ante, while in reality pushing the problem into an ill-defined and distant future. That craving for stability has now been dramatically interrupted by populism and ecological protest mediated via consumer technologies.

At frequent points in history, it has looked like a new disorder was taking the world by surprise. Yet order, supposedly disrupted, was always a mirage. Faith in the novelty of networks and the assumption that complexity was somehow new are what render the historical permanence of transnational flows, protests across civilizations, and the mutations of pandemic exchange surprising.[14] Our maps help shape the way we search for permanence in the face of impermanence. Yet it is our maps that deceive us. Complexity has always been the rule, to be found in every formation—cognitive, technological, genetic, cultural, institutional, political, and global.

Writers from Hannah Arendt to Walter Benjamin, and E. H. Carr to Gilles Deleuze, have observed that historians are the map-makers of their times. Maps help us understand our place in history; they make sense of the Zeitgeist through consciously distorted lines on the page.[15] We know our understanding of the present relies on 'shortcuts' and 'short-hands' which are inevitably faulty in some way.[16] And that these shortcuts frame our attempts to identify challenges and organize responses to them in world politics. Yet maps do more: from them, we intuit how things work and how we can figure out those workings, and make claims about what is needed to govern the world of modern politics. They are not simply errors, born of bias or a limited outlook. Our maps of the state and network seek to record the vertical and horizontal processes that are the warp and weft of reality. They express an urge to capture the basic mechanics of contemporary life. But our maps also conceal; they refract the way intersecting vertical and horizontal processes construct modernity and, so, offer misleading answers to the pressing political challenges of our time.

Inasmuch as maps express a desire to capture the basic logics governing the nature of things, we all too often fall into the trap of prioritizing one mapping over others, claiming it to be a truer reflection of our time. The common failing that comes from our attraction to mapping is not recognizing that it is the messy interaction between our maps and the vertical and horizontal logics they contain which shapes the world. Maps express a hope to represent accurately and, in the same gesture, capture universal rules of life, politics, and governance. Consequently, mapping is part of every attempt to think about our present, identify challenges, and organize political responses to those challenges. Our maps are literally entangled with the world we see.

For that reason, *unmapping* matters. Only by unmapping do we find a tool for seeing into a global future made up of interwoven logics and representations, with the hope we might navigate the 21st century more deftly than we negotiated the last. By focusing on the relationship between two maps—the network and the state—this book explores how ideal maps of the present are deployed by diverse actors—from militaries and governments to social movements, insurgents, and religious diasporas—who organize their actions in world politics today, or have done so in the past. The political implications of mapping are revealed in the following chapters where governments and their challengers variously use both the network map and the state map to represent the world and respond to it. For actors of all kinds, these maps create traps and pitfalls to understanding what drives political events. These traps call not for building new or better-quality maps or charts. Rather, they demand an unmapping to reveal how the maps themselves play out in the world around us.

Was the past truly more regular, more predictable than today? Was there ever a time when neat effects followed simple causes, when political order was easy to create and understand? When the state could govern and networks had yet to corrode its reach?[17] To ask these questions is not to doubt that modernity is beset by troubles, carrying the echoes of past traumas into the present. Certainly, this book offers no Panglossian riposte to fears for our young century. Instead, it describes the patterns that reveal how to read the present and navigate modern turbulence to help us better respond to what is unforeseen, unpredictable, and yet to come. The global politics of mapping, this book argues, plays out between two competing visions of the order of things and the human place in history. By drawing attention to how the maps of the network and state overlay and relate to one another in the minds of governments, insurgents, terrorists, social movements, and revolutionaries, there is no suggestion that one map deceives us less than the other. Overlaying the network map onto 21st-century life hides the presence of hierarchy and vertical integration running throughout every network, just as every state formation remains permeated by networks.

Making better sense of world politics requires unmapping—that is, rethinking the relationship between mappings, as part of all events, processes, and histories. Our mental images struggle to give structure to the tangle of hierarchical and horizontal logics because they fail to discern the interaction between mappings as the overriding process at work.

Networks do not follow hierarchies in history. Rather, networks engage with hierarchies to form the lines of the 21st century, just as they shaped all centuries that went before. The 'new normal' that weaves together 'distant sites' is not new at all.[18] In recognizing the boons and banes of technologies, the impacts of financial markets, the conflicts conducted through information, and the surveillance that has infiltrated social media, we must be wary of presuming that complexity is a recent innovation.[19] In short, there is little new about complex networks, and they belong to a global rather than a European-centred modernity.[20]

Maps do not just offer another lens, frame, or image of unsettled times. They represent intersections of static borders or webs of connectivity while seeking to capture the fundamental organizing logics which make up this world. Unmapping means to deny primacy to either logic and so obscure how networks and states are endlessly interacting one with the other. Only unmapping the 21st century between the network and the state can capture the play between representation and process in forming contemporary world politics.

When all that is said, perhaps something is, after all, new in our time. Increasingly visible transformations of today's nation states demand better modes of reflection on how states and networks have always been interconnected—but more than that, folded together and overlapping.[21] Thinking the present requires setting aside our faith in these maps to explore how contradictory processes of organization have always been woven together. This process is why history never repeats itself. To reflect on what the future holds demands charting lines that cut across these maps. In each part of this book, the meeting of networks and hierarchies constitutes the background conditions for the disturbance that characterizes the present.[22]

Unmapping shows how national borders and vertical linkages that cut up the world arise alongside and out of dynamic global flows and how networked and decentralized organizations carry within them logics of hierarchy and organization. Unmapping reveals the integral relationship between how humans imagine borders or diffuse political formations and how they create organizations to govern the material reality of world politics.[23] Maps deployed by various actors in world history, from terrorists to technologists, are folded together in the concrete institutional, material, social, and political processes shaping today. These are the conditions redrawing the lines of the 21st century. This book weighs the problem which the coronavirus has exposed. It explores the limits of maps to explain today's disturbed reality. Unmapping pulls apart the lines of these maps, revealing how networks and hierarchies are co-created and continue to co-create in the 21st century. Only unmapping can discover worlds yet to come: this book sets out a new cartographic tool for pioneers of the 21st century.

**Figure 1.1:** *Map of Nowhere*

Source: © Grayson Perry; courtesy the artist and Victoria Miro

# 1

# Taking the Lines Off the Map

Maps have always spoken of the status of monarchs, the power of nations, and the emergence of modern states. They project the common sense of the world and locate the cartographer's patron as the subjective actor at the centre of all things temporal, spatial, and spiritual. World maps, in particular, tend to speak of military reach, trade, economic success, and population distribution, and to bristle with pretensions to pomp and majesty.[1] Their perspective is determined from on high and so inherently suggests a politics of hierarchy.

The potter Grayson Perry's *Map of Nowhere* (2008) takes a 13th-century *mappa mundi* and employs the conventions and ideas of earlier thinkers like Leonardo Da Vinci and Thomas More to give a new sense to his world. Perry says, 'I wanted to make a map of the beliefs, headlines, clichés, and monsters that populate my social landscape.'[2] He inserts a vignette of a whirlpool at the top of the image, which he calls the 'Baloney Generator': 'describing our brain's desperation to make sense of the world and its often spurious rationalizations of our intuitive behaviour. Perhaps this map is an attempt to chart a meandering journey through my own psyche and contemporary life.'[3]

This gives us a clue to what we should be looking for when we think about maps. Maps shape the perception of contemporary life. But maps produced by states and international institutions construct social meaning: they make things look like they have always been this way. Henri Lefebvre asks: '*Is not the secret of the state, hidden because it is so obvious, to be found in space?*'[4]

The mobile phone camera with its disposable image is the latest phase of personal image capture. The democratizing age of photographic consumerism began with the daguerreotype and Victorian portrait. Preserving the image of the individual or family would echo an indication of economic and social status. It became an advertisement or statement for effect of family unity and place in the community. But it was a memento too that offered a sense of continuity and lineage to an otherwise hard life of work and toil. At the same time, it represented part of a consumer trend: it was a consumable acquisition, a commodity. It announced you could afford to have your picture taken in a photographer's studio. While 19th-century life may well have been one of hardship, it was not without its pleasures and moments of levity. These could be cherished over and over again with friends and neighbours.

Even today, to have one's photo portrait taken professionally is not cheap, albeit more widely the photo has come to represent something different today, something instantaneous and disposable. And to have a portrait painted holds a different place in our perceptions. Centuries ago, only monarchs and aristocrats could lay claim to such extravagance, and then with the aim of achieving multiple effects on the viewer. The public image as painting, even for the privileged few at court able to see it, was intended to be a revelatory experience. It should be no less shocking or awe-inspiring to courtiers than stained glass windows in mediaeval churches, backlit by the sun and burning with the fire of Christ and the Holy Spirit, were to ordinary peasants and supplicants, investing fear and submission into their minds. Power and prestige shine from every brushstroke in paintings like Hans Holbein's famous portrait of England's King Henry VIII—an unambiguous representation of a monarch at the height of his powers. The history of portrait painting aligns with political and economic expressions of power.

Maps fulfil an almost, but not quite, identical role. States demarcate their borders according to so-called Westphalian principles, and these limits are recognized, indeed sanctified, within the international community of sovereign states. Lines on a map are legal divides that states attempt to translate onto the ground in order to demarcate space, with its concrete consequences. Thus, space equates to delimiting power and identifies the ambitions of those who would extend that power by force onto neighbouring states. Just as we decipher portraits, so too can we decode maps. They are often expressions of emerging national identity, usually portrayed through the filter of charismatic leadership and a state's hegemony.

Lefebvre recognized mapping as essential to the historical production of physical space.[5] The production of a social space also requires mapping

> an edifice of hierarchically ordered institutions, of laws and conventions upheld by 'values' that are communicated through the national language. This social architecture is the state itself, a pyramid that carries at its apex the political leader – a concrete abstraction, full of symbols, the source of an intense circulation of information and messages, 'spiritual' exchanges, representations, ideology, knowledge bound up with power.[6]

But the state also exists as a 'mental space'—that is, as an imaginary. Our idea of what a state is must not be confused with its mappable physical and social spaces, but cannot be separated from them either.[7]

Maps are the means by which a state binds together its physical, social, and imaginary dimensions. In early maps describing the opening up of the New World in the early 1500s, to the south lies terra incognita, the as yet unexplored territory that would become Brazil. A century later, maps of the same region reveal the fate that awaits those who would bring trade and civilization to the interior of what had become colonial Brazil. Settlements stretch along the coast and rivers that intersect the vast interior where cannibalism was supposedly practised by a variety of indigenous tribes. These maps charted the spread of plantations into the interior, with sugar cane being delivered to the mill by its slave labour force, and detail of the civilizing mission allied to capitalist expansion, through the triangular trade which brought that slave labour from Africa to the Americas; the shipping of their products—sugar, cotton, tobacco back to Western Europe; and the further transport of cotton manufactures and other consumables to African trading ports. Colonial maps show the incremental expansion of economic markets, the extension of empire and colonies, and the layering of networks and flows as the state began to operate in global space.

## The Millionth Map

In the early 20th century, a radical project was launched by geographers. In 1913 an international conference of 35 countries declared its aim to produce the Millionth Map—a map of the entire world drawn to a scale of 1:1,000,000. A project within a project would emerge. By the early 1920s, Isaiah Bowman, Harvard scholar and eminent head of the American Geographical Society, had embarked on an 'independent but cooperative', mammoth undertaking to map 20 million square kilometres of land and coast that lay below the Mexico–US border. In effect, this attempt aimed to capture accurately on paper the United States' so-called Latin American backyard. The cost of production at the prices of the day was an astronomical half a million dollars. The work would require seven workers occupied for every day for 25 years. The Millionth Map would stretch across 107 pages; this was no simple scholastic venture. Geopolitics lurked prominently in this project to bring the countries of the Americas, central and south, under the order of state cartographers.

The First World War accelerated production of the European segment for politico-military reasons. And similar imperatives drove the United States' own regional enterprise forward. Bowman's venture played out against the background of European capital being withdrawn from Latin America to fund the war effort in Europe. Meanwhile, economically, the United States was pushing to replace European networks of ownership and so secure access to mineral, energy, and rubber commodities extraction in the region. Washington's simultaneous efforts to build bridges into the Latin American middle classes and political elites was seen as paramount if the United States was to counter a wave of nationalism that had begun to affect all strata of those societies. A dinner at the Rockefeller Center attended by Washington's finest heard Bowman describe the venture as drawing 'a continent and a half out of a state of cartographic disorder into one of order'.[8]

*To map* doesn't just mean *to know* the world: a mariner navigates the high seas or skirts the coastline; a merchant is versed in where to trade exotic goods. Nor is it merely a way of charting terrain to know your enemy on the battlefield of land or sea. Nor is it simply a way of recording population distribution and migration. Cartography captures a continuing process where we, the viewer, associate the scientific Enlightenment with state power. It is the conceptualizing of global space and its creation as an imagined space. Consequently, the world had to be ordered, brought under control of a scientific imagination and made to conform to mathematical principles of measurement and cataloguing. This went beyond elementary political marketing of a state or providing land and sea routes for entrepreneurs and traders. Early *mappa mundi*, such as the Venetian Andrea Bianco's in 1436, warned of fearsome dragons at the edge of the world as well as showing the locations of Paradise. But the newly imagined space conveyed something altogether more awe-inspiring when placed in the hands of merchants eager to open up new markets to capital.

Relations of bounded state and global networks, represented though mapping, were unfolding across European states as feudalism gradually and unevenly gave way over decades and centuries to capitalism. Where once villagers tried to preserve their self-contained worlds, so the unfamiliar world was being invited into that familiar space. For the best part of a thousand years, petering out around the 19th century, feudal villagers in England would perform a ceremony known as 'beating the bounds'. They would proceed with the ceremony once a year around the perimeter of the parish, which was marked by a series of boundary stones or boulders.[9] Inside the bounds were to be found the social relations, the loyalties, fealties and customs, and the legacy of every previous generation—a world that was known, predictable, reliable, secure, and unthreatening. Outside, beyond the bounds, lay the unknown, the threatening, the dangerous. Parishioners would process ritually from stone to stone around the perimeter, where they would occasionally pause, ritually lift a child, turn them upside down, and carefully press the child's head against the stone. This ensured the traditions of the community would transfer from the soil into the bodies of the next generation.

The modernizing space of state builders allied with capitalist entrepreneurs throughout these centuries was invading the secure space of local timelessness, destabilizing it in order to create a new temporal and spatial order of social relations. Maps were instrumental and conceptual tools with which to achieve this change, dividing and reordering common land. Instrumental in that they communicated state power into each space, encouraged exploration and travel to unknown parts, and guided home safely men and riches; but also conceptual in that they imposed a mental matrix, shifting the eye of the imagination from the village confines to a world that could now be envisaged in its entirety, then rendered controllable and subjected to being parcelled into units of property ownership under principles of accountancy and audit.

Dividing and parcelling were to become the visible tools of imperialism which exported modernity out of Europe. The Sykes–Picot line that separates Iraq and Syria was drawn up in a secret pact between the cabinets of France, Britain, and Russia in 1916 by Mark Sykes, a British foreign office official, and François Georges-Picot, a French civil servant. Ironically, Sykes signed off in pencil while Picot left a more permanent mark in ink. The intention was to divide up areas of influence in Arabia: north of the line, Syria accruing to France and south, Iraq to Britain.[10] These would delineate the lines of future geopolitical power.

Straight lines intersected ethnic, tribal, and sectarian communities. Nevertheless, a century on, Sykes–Picot continues to be recognized, unrevised, by Syrian and Iraq state elites and the United Nations. To unpick the border agreement, as the short-lived Islamic State in Iraq and the Levant sought to do, was to risk creating a precedent for other inter-state and supra-state disputes, thus unsettling the bigger picture of global stability attached to the map. Today, Russia is stretching its own borders to annex or, as Russia sees it, claim back Crimea and other territories from sovereign Ukraine and to reabsorb what it considers to be rightfully its own. Simple lines are central to the imaginary space of states, but they also create a space of vulnerability.

## The insurgent map

Revolutionaries and insurgents impose an alternative map onto the prescriptions of the state, just as the Islamic State in Iraq and the Levant sought to. All states comprise both urban and rural spaces. These two dimensions of human settlement merge, creating interstitial phases. In the same way, state borders are multivalent. They are porous, culturally diverse, and particular, displaying conditions for both permanence and impermanence. City planning shows how this is reflected in strategic social engineering. State power is mapped directly onto populations. Urban architecture and roads control the direction and speed of flow. They impose order by halting progress, by redirecting movement and will, and by accelerating certain privileged actors while slowing others.

According to Paul Virilio, for women and men caught up in the acceleration that is the prime characteristic of modernity, '[t]he manoeuvre that once consisted in giving up ground to gain Time loses its meaning: at present, gaining Time is exclusively a matter of vectors.'[11] By 'vectors', he means it's all down to the lines along which people, vehicles, and ideas and images travel, be they roads or cables. In the city, time and speed dominate over space and permanence. Insurgency strategy follows the same pattern. If you can outmanoeuvre and outrun state forces by exploiting the wide-open spaces of the countryside, then you buy yourself time. Time to fight another day.

We invest spaces with utopian longing. We yearn to rediscover the village in the metropolis, to humanize what has been taken away, to customize places to our wants and needs at a particular moment. These acts of resistance seek to mitigate the constraints imposed by the state. Space is regulated through planning and construction, through economic segregation between public and private housing, between residential, commercial and industrial use, and between the values attached to property ownership. It is controlled through monitoring and directing traffic, through electronic surveillance, and through security presence on the streets and rapid response policing. And within this web of dos and don'ts, we personalize space that has been prescribed before we even arrive there. Place, after all, is only space intersected by time.

The struggle at ground level is to impose an insurgent order on the existing order, to challenge the state with an alternative, subversive common sense. By dropping a new map on top of the old, life begins anew, recalibrating the power relationship. The state map is only one in a kind of club sandwich of maps built up over time. Insurgent powers seek to overlay new maps on the territory.

The idea of redesigning and reconstructing Paris predates the 1789 revolution by a century or more. The philosopher Voltaire noted: 'The center of the city, obscure, dense, hideous, is an example of the most shameless barbarity.'[12] The idea of rebuilding the chaotic, unplanned, organic growth of cramped and squalid paupers' dwellings alongside burgeoning commercial properties, stately monumental palaces, and prosperous houses was not new. Urban planners and urban intellectuals (like Mercier and Delamere) realized the need for a holistic reordering of the city. Change wasn't just about improving the aesthetic, beautifying the appearance of streets within a planned layout. The capitalist impetus saw the potential for knocking down poor areas in the centre, removing the population, and building long boulevards with shops, restaurants, and apartments for a growing and grateful middle class, loyal to the state. But the state also saw the chance to improve efficiency, access, and fast movement, both for promoting commerce and for providing more effective policing of any social unrest. When the self-styled Baron Haussmann was commissioned by Louis-Napoleon III to renew Paris in the 1860s, a great cross was superimposed on the new city plan. It would 'cut through the middle of the city … and bring its extreme limits at the four cardinal points, into almost direct communication'.[13] As important, it would draw the key military barracks closer together.[14]

Strategic streets were constructed. In revolutionary June 1848, the Canal Saint-Martin had acted as a defensive barricade, protecting the disorderly, often riotous neighbourhoods in the east. It was a stronghold of resistance and could delay the incursion of state forces by a week. Haussmann chose to build a new boulevard running north over the canal by lowering the depth of the canal. Thus he not only removed the barricade but also ran a conduit directly through and into the hotbed of resistance, the heart of insurgent strength. Similarly, the new Boulevard Voltaire encircled Faubourg St Antoine, a district famous already in the 1789 revolution for its riots and barricades. The aim was to isolate dangerous neighbourhoods, sever them from their local connections and support networks. Some of these would remain untouched within the confines of new major arterial roads, creating no-go zones sanctioned by security services. One such neighbourhood, Belleville, 'became a zone unpenetrated by boulevards or police, unregulated by the government, a neighbourhood where "unruly passions and political resentment held the upper hand"'.[15] So where they were not intersected for speedy and efficient military access, districts were ring-fenced and isolated as no-go zones.

As Virilio saw it, the map is inherently political. For Friedrich Engels, commenting on revolutionary Paris of 1848, the street was the locus of politics: 'the first assemblies take place on the large boulevards, *where Parisian life circulates with the greatest intensity*'.[16] The Nazi propagandist Joseph Goebbels, surveying revolutionary Berlin in 1931, addressed street-level contests for territory between Nazis and Marxists. He says: 'Whoever can conquer the streets also conquers the State!' Nazi insurgents quickly understood the politics of the street. In the early 1930s, before winning constitutional power in 1933, the insurgent Nazi grip on cities at a local street level was tenuous. They struggled to hold terrain against their fierce rivals, the Communist activists. To this end, the German National Socialists allocated a *Blockwart*—a party man, a local resident trusted with being an observer—on each city block with about 50 households. The *Blockwart's* job was to act as a gatherer of intelligence in a network of surveillance and control that ultimately reached up a hierarchy to a district leader—the *Kreisleiter*. This system was intended to impose party control over the street.[17] It was a defensive, negative measure of top-down supervision. It was good for gathering intelligence on opposition movements like the Communists, but poor at mobilizing working-class support for the party.

The problem for the state is how to penetrate and oversee the emergence of dissent that arises from social grievance. Movement within any terrain demands particular, local, home-grown street knowledge, which is always changing organically. Political organization emerges in those spaces where workers naturally agglomerate, such as the factory, or in neighbourhoods out of immediate reach of state prohibition, where measures such as limits on the use of urban space, rights of public assembly, or collective mobilization are hard to police. These are heterotopias—spaces of opposition and otherness. They connect to utopias—idealized, as yet unrealized spaces. For Henri Lefebvre, revolution emerges from a moment of 'irruption', when groups suddenly see, 'if only for a fleeting moment, the possibilities of collective action to create something radically new'.[18] Sociologist Aristide Zolberg identifies the 'moment of madness', when all things seem possible and 'politics bursts its bounds to invade all of life'.[19]

The Russian Revolution of 1917 was rooted in the factory. St Petersburg (then Petrograd) and Moscow had some of the biggest in the world at the time, bigger than Henry Ford's automobile factories in Detroit. The Russian Revolution of 1917–23 played out across heterogenous spaces. But, as Leif Jerram notes, the revolutionaries redrew a new map of the city, a new patchwork quilt centred in the factories. Revolutionary dynamics rewrote industrial schedules and workers' shifts.[20] The Bolsheviks directed many of their operations, inter alia, from the Putilov iron foundry, the country's largest artillery producer and Petrograd's biggest factory (29,000 employees in February 1917),[21] the Trubochnyi Zavod pipe factory (18,942 employees in January 1917),[22] and the Baranovski mechanical pipe and shell factories.[23] Petrograd's factories not only disrupted production schedules through wildcat strikes, but also resisted military intervention by Kornilov's Cossack troops by sending out workers organized into Red Army units to strengthen fortification detachment units and groups of agitators to infiltrate and disrupt Kornilov's troops. At the same time, they used the cannon workshop of the Putilov factory to manufacture 300 heavy artillery pieces to support the resistance. The key was to control popular support inside the workshops. These would then become the repository of nascent, parallel state institutions—soviets or committees—run by factory workers.

Just as the Paris Communards had established a rival state in the faubourgs, and as Mao had set up a shadow state in JiangXi, so the Bolsheviks, Mensheviks, and Social Revolutionaries challenged the state and each other inside factory workshops to carve out new alternative spaces within the map of state. Amid the anarchy of revolution, with central state control imploding, an absence of coordinated command and control in the military and inadequate intelligence meant state troops were slowed down when penetrating the labyrinthine industrial space.[24] What held the workshops together was local social solidarity: each workshop drew on a labour force of rural migrants—illiterate and unskilled peasants, not urbanites—who were bound together by their origins in the particular regions where their families still lived.

The notorious Bloody Sunday killings in Northern Ireland took place in Derry's Bogside in 1972 amid the terraced streets with their rows of back-to-back housing and grey uniformity. These working-class Republican strongholds offered an insurgent terrain hostile to the map of state. What this urbanscape provided was a crowdsourced distribution system, a network based on community loyalty and common identity through which Provisional IRA (PIRA) information could pass at high speed. Residents not only reported on patrolling British forces as they passed down streets—observed by so-called 'twitchers' peeping out from behind their net curtains—they also disposed of clothes and weaponry among different households as troops gave chase to PIRA snipers. In such communities, escape routes through backyards and back alleys, and via passages knocked between attics in adjacent houses, offered run-ways—or vectors—where militants could outrun hot pursuit and evade house-to-house searches, stalled by householders pleading ignorance of the unfolding events or their participants. The newly revised, local insurgent map did not respect the channels of movement that had been laid out by the original city planners and builders. The insurgent reinterpreted local space and undrew the lines of the map.

The Israel Defense Forces (IDF) would apply the same principle and draw a new counter-insurgent map in 2002 during the Al-Aqsa Second Intifada. It would find its own solution to the friction of housing and street layout. In an interview with the forensic architect Eyal Weizman, one Brigadier General, Aviv Kochavi, called it 'inverse geometry': Israeli troops called it 'walking through walls'.[25] The strategy targeted the West Bank city of Nablus, where hundreds of Palestinian guerrillas were manoeuvring around and evading thousands of IDF soldiers due to the density of housing, beyond even the reach of aerial surveillance. It involved re-conceptualizing what a city map was supposed to look like. Instead of moving through streets and alleys and courtyards that normally prescribe and regulate the flows of urban movement, Israeli forces chose to blow holes through the sides of houses, creating new points of access and egress. Drawing de facto new lines of movement between these, they created a brand new topography. New pathways were driven through what previously were walls that separated bedrooms from living rooms and kitchens, and the inside private world of the family from the outside public space, thus shaping a new city map.

The IDF attack on Jenin refugee camp in April 2002 saw Israelis impose a counter-insurgent map onto another insurgent map, which in turn overlaid the original organic map of the state-sanctioned settlement. In effect, there were three superimposed maps. Israeli troops were moving through walls to confront Palestinian fighters, who too were moving through walls but via their own informal passageways between houses, which they had created before the counter-insurgent strike. Meanwhile formal entrances to buildings, windows, and stairwells had been booby-trapped by Palestinians with explosives. One Israeli soldier described it like this:

> We never left the buildings and progressed entirely between homes
> … we carved out several dozen routes from outside the camp into its
> centre … we were all – the entire brigade – inside the homes of the
> Palestinians, no one was in the streets … we hardly ventured out. …
> We had headquarters and sleeping encampments in these buildings …
> even vehicles were placed in carved out areas within homes.[26]

The inside world of the home was turned into the outside world of the
street.[27] Maps are invested with power by the state, but the nature of a state is
also constituted by its maps. The lines on the map are subject to change both
by sovereign states and counter-state challenges. Beneath the demarcations
of the map of the sovereign, individuals and communities continuously
redraw the lines that reflect their existence in networks that broadly comply
with the state, resist the state, or, like natural forces, behave as if the state
were not there at all.

**Figure 2.1:** The empire of Ghengis Khan at his death (1227)

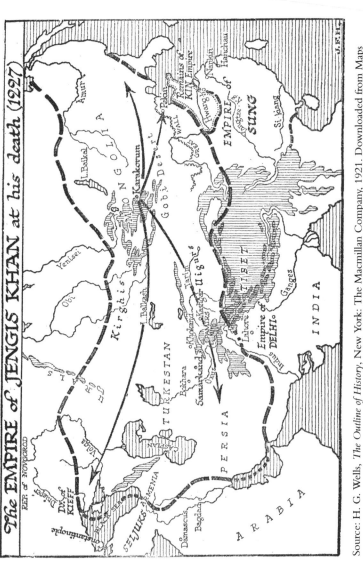

The EMPIRE of JENGIS KHAN at his death (1227)

Source: H. G. Wells, *The Outline of History*, New York: The Macmillan Company, 1921. Downloaded from Maps ETC, on the web at http://etc.ust.edu/maps [map #03656]

# 2

# A Great Unmapping

Our 'coexistence with environmental disturbance'[1] has been a regular theme in historical representations of invasions that swept from the steppes of Central Asia and East Asia into modern-day China and Europe in the early decades of the 13th century AD.[2] As early as Montesquieu in the 18th century, a conviction began to emerge that the harsh weather on the steppes had created an unusually hardy people. This trope has since been developed in a variety of ways, as Frank McLynn notes in his synthesis of literatures.[3] Some claim arid periods on the steppes at times favoured nomadic over sedentary life, leading to a dissemination of migrant horsemen in search of fresh grazing land.[4] Others suggest climatic events in surrounding areas led to widespread flooding, weakening surrounding states and rendering them vulnerable to invasion. Alternatively, it is suggested that a cool, wet period on the steppes led to a boom in grass production and an increase in horse and human population.[5] It is a curiosity of historiography that weather cycles are often seen to have played a role in setting conditions for the flows of war-making that have swept across borders of administrative power.[6] Artistic representations of the Mongols to today's Western mind reflect dark ecological visions that resonate in our own era, envisioned as a murderous flood. Such an unforgiving force, it seems, can only have had natural causes, so sudden, so complete was its destructive unmapping of all neighbouring developed states.

With the fealty of a population of around two million, living between Lake Baikal and the Gobi Desert, Ghengis Khan had constructed a war machine such as the world had not yet seen. To achieve it, he had transformed the social structure of the steppes, breaking up individual tribes, then recoalescing them into new forms and distributing them across Mongolia and beyond. This echoes with late modern European state-building, but barely fits the same mould. Marie Favereau talks of Khan's western portion of the Mongol's equestrian empire, referred to as the 'Horde', as 'neither a conventional empire nor a dynastic state, even less a nation-state ... [it] was a flexible regime, able to adapt to internal changes and external pressures'.[7] Rather, it seems to have been closer to insurgent mobilization, breaking up the clan system and remoulding it around a new military architecture.

The inhabitants of the steppes had previously moved in small parental groups, camping in associations of 50 to 100, divided into culturally distinct clans. Intertribal alliances were not new, but had been contingent on specific campaigns with a division of loot and so were generally fragile.[8] This had resulted in a social system that was flat and equal, in which multitribal dynasties had little chance of forming. In militarizing the social order, Ghengis Khan instituted multitribal units, whose leaders always sent a son to the khan's private guard (doubling as a hostage). Over time, this private bodyguard gradually became an administrative body for the entire territory, in which the key families thus all had a stake. This multitribal military elite took shape at the same time as a centralized bureaucracy. Later, kinship structures, granting hereditary roles to the Great Khan's sons, would be layered on top of this bureaucracy.[9]

If this resembles state-building, it is far from the imagined states which have dominated European history. The machine the Great Khan built was decentralized from the outset. While transforming the nomadic social structure of the steppes, there was a curious re-inscription of the nomadic form. Militarizing society was not a break with Mongol life. Rather it re-modulated existing identity. After reintroducing kinship into the leadership structure of his army/society, the Khan created a system of Ulus, each led by one of his four sons; he assigned them land not by dividing existing property, but by setting *directions*. Each son was assigned a trajectory that extended as far as their horses could reach. This method of granting land established a model of permanent conquest, an endless outwards motion. The armies had to fund themselves. Each Ulus was a spark for conquest. Having organized the tribes of the steppes into a war machine, the Khan invested them with a permanent outward motion.[10] They would traverse vast territory in an extraordinarily short time before settling into empires run by each of the Great Khan's sons. While the lines resettled in time, Mongol invasions were defined primarily by a great unmapping, stretching from China to Eastern Europe.

Visual representations of this global unmapping have historically been naturalistic. The appeal of naturalistic metaphors chimes with orientalist tropes. Yet the inherent role of war in the Mongol economy built by the Khan provides some grounds for naturalist metaphors: Perpetual conquest was necessary to feed the war machine. Ghengis Khan created a social model that was akin to a permanent, self-perpetuating revolution. Unable to tax his soldiers, the only way to sustain the Horde was to conquer territory. As McLynn puts it, the army was like 'a shark'. It had to keep moving and expanding through powerful state formations surrounding the steppes.[11]

Expansion established a tribute system that continuously channelled money and slaves back to the centre. The war machine reached as far as Central Europe, eating everything in its path.

This was something different from the birth of a European-style state. This is often forgotten because the Mongol invasion created states of a relatively traditional kind, or rather four distinct empires, as the Khan's sons split conquered territories between them. In the end, the Mongols embraced a sedentary life, and with it, the meritocratic equality of an illiterate, nomadic society was replaced by the emergence of traditional, landed, hierarchical elites. The Mongols borrowed from everywhere, being both culturally and legally parasitic. Control would remain decentralized, but where they settled, they adopted the patterns of life in the societies they had conquered, Chinese ways of life in particular. The Mongols never created a state; their mobile lines collapsed into one.

## The cycle of forms

The state is seen as the centre and origin of modern history, divided into geographic places bound to national identities. We privilege the state in our histories because we believe it to be one of the markers of historical progress, taking us towards the ideal form of political organization that shapes the present. Theory follows reality; it tries to represent it, but it also precedes and moulds it. When historical formations are categorized into proto-states, non-states, failed states, nearly states, we imply that the real state is born of necessity. Yet the state is not the only model of social organization in human experience.

Mongol invasions were not 'outside' historical progress. The sense of these events as historical oddity is perhaps why they invite explanation as a natural disaster like a flood or tsunami. The problem with modern historization is that it carries over a sense of history as progression from Newtonian mechanics. Progressive histories are stage or step histories: Marxian understandings with feudalism inevitably replaced by capitalism, which is inevitably replaced by communism; liberal understandings where religiosity is replaced by nationality, which is further superseded by the individual. Such step or stage histories are common, but they are not universal. The other face of history is cyclical or polar, involving movement, in recurrent patterns, between and across different diagrams or types of social organization. Traditionally, optimistic politics means progressive stage histories; pessimistic politics are more often bound to cyclical histories. But this does not necessarily break down on a left–right axis: neoconservatism today is a progressive stage history. Arnold Toynbee, historian and Director of Studies at Chatham House from 1925 to 1955 wrote cyclical histories. He drew from the paradigm of cyclical history associated with 14th-century Islamic historian Ibn Khaldun.

Born in 1332 in Tunis (two centuries after Ghengis Khan) to a family of migrants from Seville before it fell to the Reconquista, Ibn Khaldun was writing at the height of Islamic culture in the Mediterranean, an apogee of scientific, literary, and artistic expression. He had been active in Islamic courts in North Africa and Andalusia, but withdrew from politics to write the *Muqaddima*, or prolegomenon to world history.[12] He was interested in Islam's decline following the loss of most of the Iberian Peninsula, save for Granada. North African tribes were under threat from nomads from the east and south. Mongol invasion had shattered existing state formations to the east. Though they had eventually converted to Islam, the Mongols had ruined cities, and irrigation systems had been destroyed. As their conquest stabilized into imperial khanates, it developed oppressive tax regimes. Ibn Khaldun had met the Mongol conqueror Timur (Tamerlane), who saw himself as heir to Ghengis Khan and restorer of the Mongol Empire. Timur built an extensive empire from Persia to China. Summoned to a besieged Damascus, Ibn Khaldun saw confirmation of what would later become his thesis on sedentary and nomadic life. For him, the sedentary state was but a stage, a fleeting moment in history's endless cycle.

It comprised a stream circling between two poles of life, rising and falling eternally. History was a natural cycle between desert nomadism and sedentary, urbanized existence. Group feeling, or *assabiyya*, grew among desert tribes exposed to a harsh life, requiring people to act in unison. A powerful togetherness set in play a civilizational cycle leading to sedentary dynastic rule over urbanized life: a simple desert folk emerges with an *esprit de corps*, conquers its neighbours, and forces the conquered to submit. Religion plays a critical role in stabilizing conquered territories around charismatic leaders who found a dynasty. As the state borders expand, so the empire's wealth grows and luxury becomes possible. From that luxury and loss of harsh desert conditions develops an inevitable softening of fighting spirit and military solidarity in the conquering tribe. Military solidarity creates states; its softening leads to their decline. Increasingly, a sedentary dynasty which has lost the will to power relies on slave armies to keep order. Gradually, as the ruling dynasty becomes a burden on ruled populations, it turns to autocracy, taxation rises, and the spirit of governance declines further. Weakened by revolt, the decadent dynasty appears vulnerable to new invasion from desert nomads and the foundation of a new civilization. The rise of new, tough desert folk begins the cycle afresh. There is no progress in this vision of history, only temporary rise and fall of states with flows of nomadic warriors who settle, grow decadent, and decline. Civilization rises and falls back into nomadism. Indeed, Civilization is a function of war and nomadism. The state is the result but also the symptom and source of a decline in the nomadic and creative martial spirit. In this vision of history as process, nomads and state are bound together in an endless cycle.

Two French philosophers, Gilles Deleuze and Félix Guattari, built on Ibn Khaldun's distinction between sedentary and nomadic forms. They saw an opposition between two tendencies at work everywhere. Underlying Ibn Khaldun's story about historical cycles, they recognized an opposition between two visions of social organization—the sedentary and nomadic, the horizontal and vertical model of organization—which are represented by the map of the network and map of the state.[13]

The state organizes social life into hierarchies and structured patterns, with classes, elites, rulers, and ruled, with taxes and written laws, that organizes people together to achieve common ends like agriculture or mass production. The state is a social organization reliant on mapping space, coding and striating space with lines. It invents structures to organize people within them. Everyone knows their place, and tasks can be achieved that otherwise could not be. The state model is the imagined and hierarchical ancient city, overseen by a despotic ruler. It is an ideal 'state form', governed by a dynasty or individual which creates laws and demands obedience. This ideal city state stands in stark contrast to the nomadic way of life. Nomadic laws are fluid and locally sensitive, pragmatic and culturally mobile. Nomadic societies have elites, chieftains, and laws recorded in oral rather than written traditions. They enjoy a pattern of life, moving from one grazing area to another. Nomadic societies conform to a different model or abstract social ideal. They display greater equality and mobility or, at least, less separation between tribal elder and ordinary nomad. Organization is more horizontal and less vertical.

Nomadic chieftains retain their status when successful. Leadership is conditional on finding the best pastures and winning battles. For a chieftain, defeat leads to removal. Hierarchy is held in constant tension. Anthropologist Pierre Clastres defines some societies by the tools they develop to ward off the formation of a state and preclude the need for hierarchical order or governance.[14] His thesis suggests the map of state is unnatural, an extraordinary way of organizing social life. Top-down hierarchies are not the norm, but simply a potential tendency in human societies, since most pre-state societies had complex mechanisms for retaining relative equality in various ways. Non-state societies, Clastres argues, work to prevent a state apparatus forming. Hence they maintain more fluid and supple social systems. By contrast, the state is a rigid coding of social life. For Deleuze and Guattari, reading Clastres and Ibn Khaldun, nomadic society is the opposite map to that of the state: a radically 'non-state' society—all flow and no stability, all equality and no hierarchy, all war and no farming.[15]

Deleuze and Guattari argue that the relationship to war and conquest is one of the most significant features of nomads. Nomadic life is, in its most abstract and pure articulation, a war machine.[16] The ideal of a horde of equestrian nomads, in the spirit of Ghengis Khan or Timur, sweeping across the land, destroying and plundering all before them, constantly moving, eating up the map like an amoeba. Nomadic life is one of flows and movements, defined by release rather than containment inside lines and vertical organization of force. While state life is defined by halting, organizing, and coding social relationships in their place, in some kind of hierarchy, with a bureaucracy to give meaning to every role.

## War and revolution

Clausewitz proposes that war has an inescapable tendency towards its own purest expression.[17] It is what happens when states build war machines. The state aspires to tame the nomadic horde. Unsurprisingly, it can get out of control. Total war occurs when states lose control of their war machines—the essence of war given free rein rather than being an instrument of statecraft. Between the ideal, centralized, territorial state and the decentralized, nomadic society, there are many ways to organize social life that are neither one nor the other. All social organization may be understood as searching for a negotiated settlement between nomadism as an abstraction, and perfect, bureaucratic centralization. Accordingly, all organizations sit on a spectrum integrating the horizontal and vertical. They try to control and regulate the flows in some way, negotiating a balance between hierarchy and networked distribution.

One cannot ignore the state. It remains the most important institution in international life. But the 'ideal state' controlling its borders internally and externally, organizing life within, mastering flows that cross it and against which it defines itself is an invention, a map, and not a territory. What are understood today as sovereign states have always been integrated into networks and their movements of all kinds, covering religious transnational relations, intermarriages, cultural transmission, trade links, loans and banking. Sovereignty is always imperfect, partial, and on the edge of breakdown.[18]

Thinking the nomad requires decentring the state from history. The state is a machine for vertical mapping. States comprise processes which stabilize and seek to control the fluid movement of ideas, people, capital. The 'state' refers to different ways in which societies and elites have attempted to slow and order change, code and organize flux. It seeks to impose its cognitive map to contain flows or social forces, such as by making nomadic tribes live in settled communities. Yet fluid dynamics challenge the state's capacity to manage them with its simple map of vertical control. Sovereign borders and national identities impose order, discipline, and control on disorder that constantly breaks through. Disruptions to the map unleash unexpected effects.

Uncontrollable upswells of violence, Hannah Arendt argued, were the defining characteristic of the French Revolution.[19] But this tendency to be swept up in terror, purges, and mass executions is an essential part of revolution itself, if understood as tied to an unstoppable motion driven by the forces of history towards a rupture in time. A misplaced faith that history conceals an order waiting to break out is what paints revolution with a sinister quality. Revolution belongs to the nomad, not the state. The violence of the nomadic flood runs through revolutionary history in the form of its propensity to excess in the name of creation.

> We intend to sing the love of danger, the habit of energy and fearlessness. Courage, audacity, and revolt will be essential elements of our poetry. We affirm that the world's magnificence has been enriched by a new beauty: the beauty of speed. A racing car whose hood is adorned with great pipes, like serpents of explosive breath—a roaring car that seems to ride on grapeshot is more beautiful than the Victory of Samothrace. … We will glorify war—the world's only hygiene— militarism, patriotism, the destructive gesture of freedom-bringers.[20]

Fascist states proclaim an aesthetics and politics drawn directly from revolutionary aspects of the nomadic ideal. This should not suggest they had no grand plans for the future. The Italian diplomat and scholar Guiseppe de Michelis argued for 'World reorganization' on corporative (fascist) lines:[21] he would transfer the economic model of fascist Italy to the global level. Much like liberals of the same period, the modernist strand of fascism saw technocratic international organization as a marker of speeding technological progress. Embrace of this creative trajectory gives fascism its peculiarly aestheticized politics and capacity for violence.

Walter Benjamin notes that technological advances allowed images to be reproduced through printing, lithography, photography, and film. Consequently, art became increasingly divorced from its prior hallowed status as a symbol of elite power or ritual authority. Once the 'aura' of authenticity of the original and so unique version of a work of art was destroyed, the ability to reproduce it spawned in society a 'sense of the universal equality of things'. This produced a break in the architecture of perception Benjamin calls 'the adjustment of reality to the masses and of the masses to reality'.[22] Scope for mass participation in aesthetic expression, tied to technological acceleration, suggested that reproducing images mechanically would reveal how quantity could be 'transmuted into quality'.[23] For Benjamin, the rise of fascism depended on this process. It allowed 'the introduction of aesthetics into political life', because fascism's appeal rested on the seductiveness of mass expression made possible by accelerating technological processes of reproduction.

The rise of politics experienced *as* aesthetics could only culminate in one thing: war.[24] Reading Marinetti, Benjamin argues that fascists resolved the revolutionary potential of expression by embracing gratification through violence. The Futurists saw in war an ideal of radical novelty; it was forged in accelerating physicality, aggression, speed, and mechanics—the beauty of destruction appeared as an answer to mass progress. The political aesthetics of fascism imagined a new world forged in technological destruction. Art is democratized through reproduction, then enters into nomad history. This idea of destruction as something beautiful belongs to the left revolutionary tradition too. The anarchist Mikael Bakunin proclaims the destructive and creative urge—the urge to cast life through a prism of negativity, to celebrate violent unmapping as a road to purified politics.[25]

Imperial Germany's semi-feudal elites were central to the rise of National Socialism after the First World War and invited Hitler into power.[26] Industrialists were suspicious of democracy and saw in Hitler the promise of a return to hegemony. Established money in Germany benefited from the Nazi period: Volkswagen, Daimler-Benz, Krupp, and heavy industrial concerns in particular. Yet the reassuring story that the people were tricked by ciphered nihilists and clever propagandists[27] too easily masks the movement's genuine mass appeal. The propaganda machine certainly covered every town, city, and village in Germany. But what has been increasingly recognized is that National Socialism attracted diverse support within society as a coalition cutting across class and social fault lines. The people desired fascism.[28] They were barely tricked, but convinced by an aestheticized vision of the future—technologically utopian and dynamically violent—which carried the promise of a new agriculture, new industry, and new cities to be forged through war.

National Socialism was hyper-modern.[29] Efficient bureaucracy and modern science were necessary for the extermination of Jews, traveller communities, and the disabled. Fruits of modernization, as much a product of historical 'progress' as the airplane, show that faith in change is misplaced. In its combination of modern technology with an aesthetic of mass expression, the entire National Socialist state may be interpreted as animated by a ferocious nomadism.[30]

The most violent urges came from the street brawlers of the Sturmabteilung, whose nomadic revolutionary energetics, in the end, Hitler had to restrain, then decapitate during the Night of the Long Knives.[31] The appeal of National Socialism was rooted in a nomad aesthetic. Dispersed throughout society, it bound a hierarchical, totalitarian bureaucracy into a distributed network of informers. Tying together a charismatic central figure in Adolf Hitler and a rigid state ideology, its expressive aesthetic reached across society. The regime created a powerful urge toward the future; it promised societal rebirth.[32] A war machine ran throughout society.

Traces of this capacity for unlimited violence are identifiable in every revolutionary social movement of the left or right. Its effects are found in the Great Terror of the French Revolution, the purges of the Bolshevik Revolution, Mao's Great Leap Forward in communist China, the Killing Fields of Cambodia's Khmer Rouge, and the territorially short-lived Islamic State in Iraq and the Levant. All revolutions carry within them a nomadic machine, a flood that dreams of running free over the world. The state and nomad have always found diverse accommodations. Fascist states are but one possible arrangement.

The state is a vertical diagram for capture of all kinds of flows, such as people, trade, livestock, or agriculture. Trade leads inevitably to the breakdown of vertical organization as city states merge into banking empires. The modern state arose simultaneously with the emergence of capitalism, a machine that feeds on flux. In the 16th and 17th centuries, the state was reborn and tied into various trading networks and flows: first the Italian trading city states of Florence and Venice; then the Dutch hegemony; and then the British hegemony. But history also moves in the opposite direction, a constant degeneration from the state form which penetrates and co-creates these imperial forms and drives their global expansion.[33] Sovereignty is only claimed once the flows of capital, slaves, and markets across the world are controlled. By extending control over the seas, and the means to cross them, the state becomes a nomad state that exists in so far as it can ride out the dynamics of its networks. Imperial European states accepted they could not control all the flows. Instead they sought to make use of them—to embrace the nomad and remap themselves as global networks.

**Figure 3.1:** *Men Combined, Pukarra*, 1998 (acrylic on canvas, 200 × 163 cm)—
painting for the People of Western Australia

Source: Scott Cane, *Pila Nguru: The Spinifex People,* Fremantle: Fremantle Art Centre Press,
2002; p 99

3

# Capitalism and Imperialism

For Australia's Aboriginal peoples, lines on a map meant something different to what European elites had come to cherish. For 70,000 years, Australian Aboriginal lines did not demarcate the inside–outside borders of what Anthony Giddens calls the 'container of power' of the modern state with its divine right monarchs. Rather their lines told a dramatically different story about the land. Theirs were dreaming paths or tracks that connected directly to the Dreaming or Dreamtime—the origins of time. They criss-crossed a land mass bordered only by the oceans. These were the routes taken at the beginning of time by totemic ancestors who sang out the names of the animals, rocks, and waterholes they encountered. Thus, they sang the world into existence. And each section of each route still has attached to it a story of creation, history, and resources remembered in stories, songs, and rituals. Europeans call them Songlines; Aboriginal peoples call them 'the Way of the Law'.[1] They form part of an oral history of map-making. A person walking along them intersects different stories, different language and family groups. Hence Myers explains: 'the mythological personages of the Dreaming travelled from place to place, hunted, performed ceremonies, fought, and finally turned into stone or "went into the ground", where they remain. The actions of these powerful beings—animal, human, and monster—created the world as it now exists.'[2] Knowledge of the ancestors and their movements is not open to question or theorizing. It is so because it always has been so. And knowledge is passed on according to one's progress in society and accession through age.[3] It is not objectified like Western cultural knowledge or philosophy. Rather, it is lived through repeated ritual and practice that provides a continuity with the ancient, timeless past and endless future.[4] These mythological heroes of human and animal form are alive. In their travels, they have left behind them physical and symbolic landmarks—rivers, mountains, trees, waterholes. Land and mythological heroes are one. The network of tracks across Australia represents not only the tracks of mythological heroes but also the selfsame paths that contemporary

Aboriginals walk in pursuit of food and marriage partners, thus reinforcing the continuity with all time. Bruce Chatwin's *Songlines* captures their essence:

> In theory, at least, the whole of Australia could be read as a musical score. There was hardly a rock or creek in the country that could not or had not been sung. One should perhaps visualize the Songlines as a spaghetti of Iliads and Odysseys, writhing this way and that, in which every 'episode' was readable in terms of geology.
>   'By episode', I asked, 'you mean "sacred site"?'
>   'I do.'[5]

The Aboriginals and their 50,000-year history have been widely understood in the context of clans and tribes of itinerant nomads. But their mappings illustrate both the diversity and dissemination of communities and the life force in the geographic spaces they dream.[6] Non-human–human networks, established as Dreamings or Songlines, pre-existed the settlement patterns that later colonists would overwrite onto the soil as property ownership. Smallpox spread rapidly throughout the indigenous population with disastrous effects following the arrival of Europeans; testament to the network of trade and communications routes already in place. The British fleet which landed in 1788 with its cargo of 548 male and 188 female convicts marked a dual incursion. It would establish, in Robert Hughes' words, 'not Utopia, but Dystopia'—one whose intellectual patrons were Hobbes and Sade.[7] Indeed it ran counter to the spirit of political revolution sweeping America and France.

This incursion created a penal colony with a 14,000-mile oceanic prison wall. At the same time, it introduced a project of colonization which would take advantage of the latticework of tracks and paths connecting Aboriginal communities known as nations and farming settlements. Far from introducing new paths of penetration into the vast land mass, the colonizers' trade, communications, and settlement patterns were to be laid over the network of routes that had existed for thousands of years and which followed natural waterholes, rivers, and valleys. What had survived for tens of thousands of years would be replaced as if overnight by a project to centralize administration with its new economy via the new colonial government in Sydney, and from this regional hub to the hub of empire in London. Robert Hughes makes the point: 'The most puzzling question for the whites, however, was why these people should display such a marked sense of territory while having no apparent cult of private property. What was it that bound them to the land?'[8] If Aboriginal Dreaming networks were bounded by the oceans, it was the oceans that would provide colonizers with the networks of early capitalism and imperial domination of the seas and foreign lands. The Western mind at this point should shake free of the ideal of fixed borders, meanings, and references, and look for pre-existing networks, flows, and the ways people lived and traded as social and political actors.

Thomas Hobbes in his *Leviathan* (1651) establishes the basic principle of the state.[9] He proposes that individuals escape the anarchy and brutishness of the state of nature by relinquishing their individual rights, pooling them in society, and investing trust in the sovereign, monarch, or leviathan who redistributes those rights to the greater common good, thus replacing disorder with a vertical order. The problem is that the natural inequalities of the state of nature—unequal strength and unequal property ownership—are carried into the Hobbesian state too. In his *Second Treatise of Government* (1690), John Locke establishes property ownership as the foundation of good government and civil society. He addresses the topic of the commons, or commonly held lands, in an abstract way. Yet he then attaches it to the contemporaneous image of America, at the time an unspoiled, untapped terrain outside the state. In Section 49, he writes, 'in the beginning all the world was America'.[10]

But the reality of a complex sociolegal feudal system of commons and estates with warranties and obligations from master to serf and vice versa is avoided by Locke. The historical reality of a shift from obedience to the local lord to responsibility to a distant state is absent from his account. Locke is disingenuous (in Section 35) when he says that 'no one can inclose or appropriate any part, without the consent of all his fellow-commoners; because this is left common by compact, i.e. by the law of the land, which is not to be violated'. For centuries, parishes in England had contained estates that were the property of the local lord and which must be cultivated and tended by the tenants of the village or parish. They also contained additional common and uncultivated wasteland. These could be farmed and pasture made available for livestock according to the needs of the community. They were also protected within long-standing institutions of common usage. According to the scholar Lewis Hyde: 'The commons are not simply the land but the land plus the rights, customs and institutions that organize and preserve its communal uses.'[11]

The system of early capitalist enclosures suggests a mental image of fencing off, hedging, or walling open land. This is a misleading picture. Common land could be fenced too. While 'several' or private land could be open. So, a legal definition offers a more useful context. By law, enclosure means 'the removal of communal rights, controls or ownership over a piece of land and its conversion into "severality", that is a state where the owner had sole control over its use, and of access to it'.[12]

The arrival in the 15th century of large-scale sheep farming for textile commodity production and trade would lead to the enclosing of common lands. This concentrated the use of space, aggregating scattered strips of arable land into larger units. Thereby it created more efficient and productive yields on investment. At the same time, England's Tudor and Stuart monarchies brought feudal lands into a broader economy of the central state. Economies produced fluctuations in the cloth market (booms and busts), which reinforced evictions from land and increased uncertainty and unemployment among the peasantry. Systematic terror campaigns and eviction from common lands that had been farmed for generations would, over time, produce an underclass of peasants without regular work and deskilled from their former occupations. These so-called masterless men were now rudderless.[13] To have a master or feudal lord was to have a predictable and reliable place in the social order. To be masterless was to be an itinerant vagabond, to become easy prey to criminal conviction in the courts. At best, to be the purveyor of mobile, human labour within an emergent system of capitalist economic class relations. In 16th- and 17th-century England, with its rapidly growing population, there was already a large mobile, yet deskilled, workforce. Simultaneously and for the first time, the idea of the 'mob', a criminal underworld, entered popular consciousness.[14] And London with its population explosion (eightfold between 1500 and 1650) became a sanctuary.

For all that Christopher Hill famously saw political motives behind enclosure, so too did his fellow Marxist historian E. P. Thompson see it as 'a plain case of class robbery'.[15] That said, enclosure remains a sorely contested concept. Common and waste lands were enclosed for different reasons. Peasants conspired in their own demise by exchanging their land 'by agreement', allowing for the 'piecemeal enclosure and the exchange of open-field strips to create consolidated holdings'.[16] This is not to deny the role of a nascent bourgeoisie, a merchant class that increasingly sought the benefits derived from commodifying not just the produce of the land but also the labour of each individual worker. The process of enclosure, once set in motion, would continue inexorably throughout the first and into the second industrial revolutions.

## Masterless men

At the heart of the new economy was a new understanding of the land and, therefore, space. Against this context, another major development was being played out. War raged between mainland European states between 1618 and the Treaty of Westphalia in 1648. Ostensibly it was a protracted conflict between Catholic and Protestant states that produced extreme and tragic consequences. Its echo would be heard three hundred years later in Bertolt Brecht's seminal play *Mother Courage and Her Children*. It is set in this period and tells of a mother of three who plies her provisions trade as a camp follower. Her fortunes rise and fall with the ebb and flow of armies that traverse Europe. Over time, she loses her children one by one yet remains existentially committed to and dependent on the continuation of war. At the same time, in England by the 1640s, civil war and revolution were being waged. The divine right of kings, embodied by King Charles I, was being challenged by Parliamentarians—representatives of a merchant class and rural yeomanry, an emergent bourgeoisie intent on redistributing the powers of state. Regicide would lead to a brief period of Commonwealth, only to be supplanted by Oliver Cromwell's military Protectorate and dictatorship.

Of significance are, one, the role of the Parliamentarian New Model Army, viewed not so much through its familiar lens as a military paradigm of organization and efficiency. Nevertheless, understood as a crucible of political and religious fervour, dissent, and ideology. Furthermore, a hotbed of millenarian and nonconformist revolution. And, two, the rapid suppression of new radical and revolutionary voices in the lower ranks of the army by its senior commanders functioning as agents of an organizing business class. Indeed, one that formed the basis of what the sociologist Max Weber would later identify as a Protestant capitalist class.

The effect was not only to entrench the influence of capital set against a traditional, aristocratic landowning hegemony. It also released onto the oceans, into the transatlantic trade, waves of masterless men and political and religious refugees and deportees as raw labour. This commercial trade served to network the high seas. It connected Africa, the Americas, and Britain in a triangular business model that at once shipped manufactures from English ports like Bristol, London, and Liverpool to West Africa, where physical goods were exchanged for human capital—slaves that would be quality graded and priced by their physical attributes for work in the plantations of the North American, Caribbean, and South American colonies. Produce in the shape of sugar, cotton, coffee, and tobacco would be shipped to English ports and sold to a growing consumer market. By 1698, Jonathan's Coffee House, in what is now a part of the City of London, offered a list of stock and commodity exchanges. This allowed returns to be made on investments: the London stock market and the insurance markets were born as organizing hubs for a global network.

As Jairus Banaji notes, commercial capital remained dominant into the late 19th century, 'when an entirely new breed of industrial capital, the capital-intensive vertically integrated firms, would finally emerge to eliminate the old-style merchants by organizing their own sales networks'.[17] Until this point, the British Empire had, like its hegemonic predecessors the Italians and the Dutch, 'encapsulated a capitalism of networks',[18] the state acting as enabler of these diffuse networks. Unlike in Fernand Braudel's reading, which describes the collapse of one into the other.[19] Vertical integration would come later in the European experience.

It was in relationship to these same networked processes that the British state would develop the world's leading maritime force, both for military and merchant purposes, in a mutually beneficial annexing of lands and trade routes for imperial control. As much as the British state was reinforcing its own national identity in the face of the other or outsider, it was also extending the notion of sovereignty to take on a new spatial conceptualization. Oceans were no longer the boundary to delimit national power of the British island state. Rather oceans became the facilitator of a networked, richly connected empire with Britain as the central hub. The lines on the map that would come to matter most were those which connected international centres of trade and commodity production.

The underclass, the masterless men exported as convicts, as well as all manner of people deemed undesirable and an array of political and religious utopians and refugees built, on these same lines, what Linebaugh and Rediker term a 'revolutionary Atlantic'.[20] Prison was a commonly applied technique of terror. In London alone, 13 'houses of sorrow' were listed. In 1553, Bridewell in London housed orphans, vagrants, petty offenders, and disorderly women. The jailed were subjected to arduous hard labour. In 1587, 1607, and 1609, Essex experienced a wave of construction of houses of correction, merging the concepts of discipline and charity. The extreme sanction was capital punishment. In 1598, 74 people were hanged in Exeter and 74 more across Devonshire.[21] The development of early capitalism became systematically invested with a culture of fear. However, the terror of having neither permanent home nor employment, and subsequently of being put to work by the court and prison system, would increasingly take on a new dimension, namely the forced supply of manpower for the army and navy. The Beggar Act 1598 provided for first-time offenders to be flogged but second-time offenders to be banished and transported. Bridewell prison provided thousands of bodies as soldier recruits to fill the galleys of an expanding maritime force. It was more productive, if not more profitable, than execution. It also sent out a signal to the unemployed to avoid idleness.[22]

Age proved no barrier. Bridewell shipped children between 8 and 16 years of age to the colony of Virginia—founded in the name of England's Queen Elizabeth I—against their will and without due authority. The Privy Council soon made amends. Yet, by 1625, the record shows that only 7 per cent of the first shipment had survived, and in 1627 a further 1,500 adolescents were shipped out. The practice would continue. In 1653, under the Commonwealth, some 400 Irish children were stolen from their beds and shipped to Virginia.[23] A whole language developed around the capture off the streets and forced removal of people to be sold to slavery in the Caribbean. These were the so-called 'spirits' who had been spirited away, nabbed, or kidnapped, in the jargon of the period that we still use today. Men were entrapped and impressed to become enforced labour and serve in the navy.[24]

Karl Polanyi's *The Great Transformation* notes the paradox in the labour market across the following centuries. In 1601, the Poor Relief Act made individual parishes responsible for footing the bill for their poor. And that included any newly arrived poor moving between parishes. In 1662, the Settlement Act set about removing the abuse that had been identified where itinerant poor were attracted to relocate to more prosperous parishes. To be entitled to live legally in a parish, one had to be born there or married into it, or meet a host of other conditions. Anyone moving between parishes needed to provide a settlement certificate vouching that the home parish would meet the cost of removal of the person from the new parish should they call on poor relief. This reduced the movement of official labour. It also began the regulation of a functioning labour market. The rules of parish serfdom were loosened in 1795. But just as a national labour market seemed within reach, so the new Speenhamland Law was introduced, reinforcing the old Tudor and Stuart paternalistic system of poor relief with its punitive conditions attached.[25] Now caught in a poverty trap, the poor, the unemployed, criminals, and criminalized would provide labour for the colonizing efforts of the state from the 16th to 19th centuries.

The 1640s witnessed a civil war in England. Only to be accompanied by an explosion of political writing and publishing as the grip of courts and censors was loosened during the tumultuous years between the outbreak of fighting in 1641 and restoration of the monarchy in 1660. These were revolutionary decades. Fragmented Protestant sects proliferated. Movement and exchange between them occurred frequently. Quakers, Seekers, Ranters, Levellers, True Levellers, Diggers, Muggletonians, Grindletonians, Baptists, Anabaptists, and Antinomians spread throughout the land. This was encouraged by radical preachers, prophets driven on and guided by an inner light that illuminated the path to attaining truth. Mechanick preachers and self-tutored prophets, to whom God had spoken directly, toured the country and addressed public gatherings in the heated language of rebellion. They defined themselves against the state Anglican Church and the existing political order. But Antinomians opposed authority in general rather than taking aim at particular parts of the power structure. Nuanced beliefs of the non-denominational sects are too varied to interrogate here. However, they ranged from millenarianism and believing in the second coming of Christ to communist land and asset distribution. Levellers espoused religious tolerance, extending suffrage, but via the supremacy of popular sovereignty over parliamentary sovereignty; True Levellers or Diggers emphasized the bond between man and nature, and common ownership; Quakers preached social and gender equality; Ranters proselytized liberal sexual practices; Muggletonians preached Christ's imminent return.

Many sects found rank-and-file sympathizers in Parliament's modern fighting machine—the New Model Army—where agitators lobbied often equally sympathetic officers. Meanwhile, at the senior level of army grandees, their commander-in-chief Oliver Cromwell agreed only so far as to extend voting rights to more populous areas of the community. As a member of the landed yeomanry from Huntingdonshire, a prime stumbling block for Cromwell was his conviction that the vote should be limited to those who owned a stake in the land. Only those who represented capital could be relied on to vote responsibly. Parliamentarian political and military elites came to represent a bourgeois class now increasingly threatened by a rebellious social underclass.

Putney, a village on the south bank of the River Thames, hosted not only an encampment of the New Model Army in 1647 but also the famous Putney debates where radical officers like Thomas Rainsborough, leader of the Levellers, and the leading Digger Gerrard Winstanley railed against the theft of the commons and the encroaching slavery of their former occupants. By 1649, grassroots revolutionaries had been silenced by Cromwell's army. The suppression of a rebellious underclass by the nascent bourgeoisie had begun. Distancing of interests between the property-owning bourgeoisie and the propertyless poor would become a recurrent theme in revolutions, from the French Revolution and throughout the 19th and subsequent centuries. The persecution of radicals would be complete with the restoration of Charles II's monarchy in 1660. With the collapse of Cromwell's Protectorate, the counterrevolution had a free hand to turn on non-denominationalists, and with a vengeance. The escape door pointed west to the Americas. Thousands of Protestant radicals were imprisoned or transported to the colonies. While others like the Quakers and Muggletonians reinvented themselves, propounding pacifism, so removing themselves as a threat to the state.

## Body commerce

The transatlantic slave trade anchored the relationship between state formation, capitalism, and colonial imperialism. Along with the criminalized peasant class and radical Protestants of the English Revolutionary Civil War who were shipped to the Americas and convict colonies like Australia, African human capital was commoditized and slaves exchanged on world markets bound for the plantations. Here they produced physical commodities for a new capital class. Richard Braithwaite was a prosperous Parliamentarian during the 1640s. 'Hydrarchy' was the word he used to describe the growing power of the British state's domination of the seas. Linebaugh and Rediker summarize: 'The seizure of land and labour in England, Ireland, Africa and the Americas laid the military, commercial, and financial foundations for capitalism and imperialism, which could be organised and maintained only through Braithwaite's hydrarchy, the maritime state.'[26] Human trafficking on which this maritime state relied was not new. Slave networks for profit between the 8th and 11th centuries connected the Caspian Sea—bordered by modern-day Chechnya and the Central Asian stans—to London. Across the Sahel, trans-Saharan networks existed since the 7th century. The North Atlantic that connected Africa, Europe, and the Americas saw its heyday between the 15th and 19th centuries, transporting some 13 million slaves.[27]

The Atlantic trade extended and mapped new maritime networks onto existing regional trade networks. European capitalists meshed their networks onto existing African and Arab trading networks. These were already engaged in buying and selling commodities, especially that defining commodity, the human body. They included human commodities moved across Africa and from the interior to the west, north, and east coasts of the continent. Traders were both African tribes and Arab merchants. East Africa's coastal towns had supplied Islamic empires with slave labour for centuries. One historian points out: 'African ivory was much needed in China and much prized in India, while in Islamic India and in Mesopotamia [Iraq] there was an insatiable demand for slaves.'[28] In Europe, for six hundred years, 'from the middle ages to the early modern period', a principal and critically important traded commodity was mercenary manpower.[29]

Portuguese traders between the 1470s and 1690s were the first Europeans to take advantage of a market in slaves. Their supply network connected West African ports such as Luanda and Benguela in modern-day Angola and transported captive Africans north by ship to the Gold Coast in modern-day Ghana. These Africans were purchased, shipped, then traded on the Gold Coast for locally mined gold before it was sent to Europe. But the Gold Coast was predominantly restricted to gold and ivory acquisition, not slave purchase, for fear of disrupting the lucrative gold trade. Further south, the Slave Coast—modern-day Nigeria, Benin, Ghana, and Togo—accounted for significantly higher slave exports to the Americas. This parochial network locked into pre-existing networks. Trade networks across the Saharan and along the Niger River system were already more sophisticated and efficient.[30]

At stake in these networks of body commerce is, to some extent, the origin of money itself as a universal measure of exchange and value. From ancient Greece and Rome, military success resulted in slaves to sell, but called for mercenaries to be paid as well. Bodies and coinage clearly corresponded. In this sense, as Robert McNally puts it, money 'emanates from the body'.[31] Commerce in slaves passed along the silk roads and maritime routes, fuelled by the growth of Muslim and Mongol empires. Trade created global networks linking Slavs, Celts, and Scandinavians to trans-Saharan slave routes over 13 centuries on a scale that may have even surpassed that of the later Atlantic slave trade.[32]

Late emergent European states captured and centred the global flow in human bodies. Forced labour of those criminalized by state judiciaries, abducted by state security agencies, or acquired by an expanding business class flowed down these channels. Their new homes would be the colonies of empire—systematic gulags or labour camps—that produced new wealth to be reinvested in the commodity and shareholder markets of the cosmopolitan centre. Viewing colonies as emergent dependencies and eventual proto-states can divert attention from the maritime networks that connected terrains and cemented distribution channels for body commodities and their manufactured products. These channels are absent from world maps, which tell only the story of sovereign self-government behind borders that are nominally, mutually respected following the Peace of Westphalia.

Oppressed and enslaved workforces would rise up against authoritarian colonial regimes and create resistance networks, feeding their ideas back into wider revolutionary processes. A succession of revolutions—American (1775–83), French (1789–99), and Haitian (1791–1804)—drew on ideas of human suffrage and democratic egalitarianism.[33] But to grasp the trajectory within these ideas, the Atlantic basin should be read as a networked space of exchange and interconnections which had commodified human bodies at its root. Nature's winds and ocean currents created a circular motion critical to sailing ships before the advent of steam mechanization. Across the Atlantic they offered a naturally powered direction of movement for cargos of trade and ideas to circulate, from Northern Europe to West Africa to the Americas and across to Europe. Conceiving the Atlantic as a multi-lane transit bordered by coastal settlement is to see a set of nodes and links within a macronetwork that further incorporates regional micronetworks capable of creating a cauldron of resistance and rebellion.

Just as in the 1640s political and religious radicals had penetrated the Parliamentarian army, so too did resistance, albeit to a lesser extent, infiltrate the navy with its press-ganged crews. The Levellers, in three landmark papers, spoke out against both the appalling conditions that sailors had to endure and the evils of impressment.[34] Such sentiments were echoed in the culture of buccaneers, corsairs, and privateers—pirates who attacked Spanish convoys in the Caribbean, often with official, sometimes unofficial, and sometimes no sanction from London. A generation before, Walter Raleigh, Francis Drake, and John Hawkins had been privateers and corsairs beholden to and rewarded by the court and grace of Elizabeth I.

Piracy both served and challenged the interests of expanding capitalist slave states. Only when it began to free itself entirely from hierarchical control was piracy suppressed by the cosmopolitan centre. Regarded as 'the outcasts of all nations'—contemporary attitudes considered them the detritus of society, from prostitutes and escaped slaves to political prisoners and religious radicals—pirates lived 'beyond the line' in the safety of Maroon communities of runaway slaves on islands and in mountains and forests. It was between these communities and the Caribbean and North American coastal towns that rebellions spread, their influence rolling back to creole settlements on Africa's west coast and farther to England and France. Rebellion would spread along the western rim of the Atlantic basin between the 1670s and late 1700s, pitting slaves against slave owners—reflecting what Sylvia Wynter terms the 'ambivalent' political, cultural, and existential rift between the network of plots (the patches of land given to the individually enslaved to feed themselves) and the racial plantation system with its hierarchical structure.[35]

Mutinies would increasingly affect Atlantic trade and shipping networks. In 1712, New York City experienced a rebellion in which 25 slaves were executed. A severe earthquake struck New England in 1727, reminding sinners they should pay greater heed to God's will. The Great Awakening of the 1730s set off a wave of evangelism and revivalism in the American colonies that recalled the spirit of English Civil War sects like the Levellers and Ranters and their proselytizing egalitarianism.[36] The West Indies witnessed successive slave rebellions in the 1730s. The Stono Rebellion of 1739 in South Carolina saw hundreds of slaves executed. In 1740, preacher George Whitefield addressed the third of three open letters in Philadelphia to 'the inhabitants of Maryland, Virginia and North and South-Carolina', colonies that had recently witnessed slave rebellions.[37] He intoned: 'considering what usage they commonly meet with, I have wondered, that we have not more Instances of Self-Murder among the Negroes, or that they have not more frequently rose up in Arms against their Owners'.[38]

The New York Conspiracy of 1741, a year after Whitefield's letters, brought together different radical strands. All played out against a background of the Anglo-Spanish War. Rumour spread that Spanish ships were already at sea, sailing to liberate New York's slaves.[39] Philadelphia's *American Weekly Mercury* talked of a 'diabolical plot' only for a series of arsons to set alight New York in March and April of 1741. The *Boston Gazette* reported the plot, which nearly burned down the 'entire town'.[40] The outcome was to be expected: 142 slaves were arrested, 72 confessed, 13 were burned at the stake, and 18 were hanged.[41]

The Atlantic slave trade was not a mere backdrop to rising chaos.[42] Coastal towns, plantations, and ships themselves became locations of resistance in networks of mobility, countering global monetary networks shaped directly out of human bodies and blood.[43] Personal identities were reforged through new connections and overlaps between ethnic groups in resistance. Black and white became increasingly fungible descriptions. Equally, it is advisable not to paint with too broad brush strokes. Ira Berlin and Philip Morgan reveal the differences between local masters' economies, impacting master–slave power relations, and the vulnerabilities and opportunities that could be exploited by slaves.[44] Man-made and natural disasters, from revolution to hurricanes, impacted commodity prices. The American War of Independence (1775–83) severed the supply lines of mainland foodstuffs to the Caribbean. Slaves on those islands suffered extreme shortages. The eventual outcome was the Haitian Revolution. Meanwhile, masters would use shortages and gluts, and the rise and falls in world commodity prices to calibrate social relations between master and slave. But as local as their effects might be, they were nevertheless located in wider, networked relations that combined the birth of early capitalism, out of colonial control and exploitation in the industrial plantation structure, with revolutionary tendencies.[45] Capitalism here appears as a revolutionary movement which emerges from yet also projects beyond slave societies, shaping the no less hierarchical and still racially structured states that followed them.[46]

Since the 16th century, Spain—the recognized global superpower at the time—had failed to restructure its economy. The Dutch, from their small territorial base but with an extensive merchant navy, by contrast, set out first to dominate international trading routes, then refined their ambitions into displacing the bankers of the city states of Venice, Florence, and Genoa, at the heart of international financial exchange. But they too would one day be challenged and pushed aside as the British first developed their own merchant and military navies to expand and protect their trading routes before placing themselves at the heart of *haute finance*—namely global banking networks— while capitalism continued to extend its tentacles to all parts of the world. Capitalism proliferated as a global revolutionary movement by weaving its logic into the expansionary ambitions of emergent European colonial slave states. This project would construct the lines on the map we recognize today. But beneath these lines on the map, the constitutive networks and flows through them would continue to thrive despite the relentless drive to cartographic hegemony.

**Figure 4.1:** Ibn Al Wardi's Mappa Mundi, circa 1349

4

# Thinking Like a State

The idea that after 1648 the world was suddenly reborn to fit a map of sealed sovereign units has lived an undeservedly long life. This myth is well understood to neglect the complexity of transnational organizations in Europe at the time and afterwards. In particular, overlapping networks of city states, monarchies, banking associations, principalities made up the Holy Roman Empire.[1] The pull of capitalism later allowed for the production of integrated national economic circuits. Nationalism, with its force that could cohere populations in a common identity, remained fragile and transient faced with global flows and connections. The ideal of statehood has always been out of step with the reality of networks.

Pierre Bourdieu notes 'when we study the state ... we risk applying to the state a "state thinking" [for] the very structures of consciousness by which we construct the social world and the particular object that is the state, are very likely the product of the state itself'.[2] The state is attractive to historians because 'it suggests the possibility of enforcing an ideal'.[3] A certain 'complicity' always implicates scientific analysis of the state.[4] The state is a map revealing the workings of all vertically integrated organizations within a discrete territory organized by compartmentalizing its command-and-control structure. Its history is one of regulating a series of flows—economic, human, or ideational. It is a machine for coding those flows. The head of state taxes transactions undertaken by merchants, and the proceeds pass up the administrative pyramid. Money is used to build ships, pay soldiers, or employ police to keep the ports open, deter piracy, ensure merchants have a safe place to dock, and order the marketplace. The state ideal may be understood to resemble the software of a computer, which arranges inputs before directing their distribution according to its vertical program.

As a map, the state is static, top-heavy, and surveils from above. No state actually matches its diagram. The closest approximation to the state ideal were the early urban and imperial formations of Mesopotamia—which, Weber argues, reduced everything to a 'uniform order'.[5] Dominated by a despotic ruler, an intrusive bureaucracy and agricultural underclass, it relied on coercion, extraction, and vertical accumulation. Organized on a 'radial axis',[6] early city states like Ugarit, Ur, and Babylon conformed to the map. Lest it be forgotten: 'Conceptually, the map has either preceded the physical presence of the city or served to regulate and coordinate its continued existence.'[7] The vertical geometry of the City Plan precedes the builders' arrival. In a literal sense, the states that arose from the first human settlements are based on the graphic system of the map.[8] In practice, these cities usually gave rise to 'proliferating authorities', merchants, and lenders.[9] But the state is a map of political verticality. At the opposite pole to the horizontal politics of the nomad, sweeping across the steppes, stopping just long enough to send back slaves and build mountains of skulls.

Centralized, vertically integrated hierarchies make for brittle structures. They excel in exercising command and control in stable conditions, but not in responding to changing conditions. A period of decline around 1177 BC led many of the early empires in Mesopotamia to collapse. The cascading implosion of Hittite, Mycenean, and Kassite kingdoms are often linked to the so-called 'sea peoples'.[10] Whatever the cause, the trading mercantile city states situated along coasts were better equipped to survive external shock than vertically integrated empires. As Josephine Quinn suggests, hierarchically integrated states were less resilient to climate change, population pressures, and economic crises, which the networked trading city states of the Levant— Tyre, Sidon, Byblos—were better able to weather.[11]

The state maps the world, categorizes, rationalizes, and striates space so as to make it legible. As James Scott notes, this 'way of seeing' sits at the heart of the many disasters of state planning, from villagization in Tanzania to the Great Leap Forward in China to collectivization in Russia.[12] Tragedy can follow from social engineering driven by the state map. Faith in maps drawn by the hand of vertical command-and-control bureaucrats, especially in authoritarian regimes intent on redesigning society root and branch, tends towards catastrophe. Where the state map meets complexity inherent in all functioning social orders, catastrophe ensues. The state is an industrial designer whose utopian hubris cannot be divorced from its attraction to oversimplification. Whether in post-revolutionary planning, in racist colonial projects, or in urban design, the map of state simplifies and invites catastrophe. What renders a system stable and resilient is disturbed and inhibited by the vertical map of state. For vertical planning is unable to manage the networked uncertainty that characterizes all ecological, social, and political dynamics.

No map simply communicates reality.[13] The map of state frames social organizations according to how far they deviate from a vertically integrated hierarchy. But what are the alternatives? Warren Magnusson develops Scott's line of thought, suggesting that cities which flourished in history were spaces where multiple centres of rule or authority were held in various allegiances, identities, overlapping networks, and hierarchies.[14] Hence 'to see like a city is to accept a certain disorderliness, unpredictability and multiplicity as inevitable, and to pose the problem of politics in relation to that complexity'.[15] If the city has its own way of seeing, which might be applied elsewhere, what of international political formations which cross fragile state borders?

## Nation of the faithful

The transnational politics of the ummah has always evaded European cartographers, whose 'cognitive map' of the nation state is delinked from imperial 'territories of extraction and subjugation'. Nowhere is that more evident than in Islamic cultural zones which are globally networked yet divided by awkward lines drawn by external powers.[16] The very shape of Europe was constituted in line with the philosopher Hegel's 'confidence that Islam was being driven back to its Oriental and African quarters',[17] and so historically alien to the state map of Europe. The legacy, Rexhepi suggests, is a failure to capture the politics of networked Islamic affiliations across the world. Transnational relations in the minds of Muslim populations 'left behind' when the borders were drawn after the fall of the Ottoman Empire endure to the present day.[18] Recoding these populations as 'foreign' under new state maps was a symptom of the European cartographer's inability to map politically the nation of the faithful.

Is it possible to make political sense of a term that defines a global community without a state? That implies an unmapping of the Middle East, Africa, and Asia? For much of the 20th century, the pan-Islamic ummah was not seen as so effective a resource as nationalism in struggles waged across the Middle East and North Africa against imperialism. Until the 1950s, a modern national state formation was deemed the most potent resource for political mobilization in the region. Faith in the state map had already been globalized through the networks of empire.

Walter Benjamin asks what *allows for* translation.[19] This question, for any conscientious translator, should be: 'Does its nature lend itself to translation and, therefore, in view of the significance of the mode, call for it?' Does the thing itself call for translation? Translatability is a quality of certain works, he argues. We are not divided, for: 'Languages are not strangers to one another, but are, a priori and apart from all historical relationships, interrelated in what they want to express.' When something is difficult to translate, this is not a question of irreconcilable linguistic rules. Translation, indeed all understanding, is never complete. The task of translation is not to transmit: 'The transfer can never be total, but what reaches this region is that element in a translation which goes beyond transmittal of subject matter.' Translation, for Benjamin, is best understood as the process of language developing. It is creative, because neither the object nor subject of translation is stable.

> No translation would be possible if in its ultimate essence it strove for likeness to the original. For in its afterlife—which could not be called that if it were not a transformation and a renewal of something living— the original undergoes a change. Even words with fixed meaning can undergo a maturing process. … [T]he greatest translation is destined to become part of the growth of its own language and eventually to be absorbed by its renewal. Translation is so far removed from being the sterile equation of two dead languages that of all literary forms it is the one charged with the special mission of watching over the maturing process of the original language and the birth pangs of its own.[20]

Peter Mandaville sees the invention of monotheism as a revolutionary idea.[21] In the 7th century, Arabia was populated by nomadic and semi-nomadic tribes. Important trade routes ran through it, linking urban nodes by caravan trails. The Prophet Muhammed was born at a key node, Mecca. The central doctrine of the oneness of God, forbidding worship of any other god, would become the defining revolutionary statement of the last two millennia. Regardless of its metaphysical content, it is a religious ideal so close as to be indistinguishable from the state map; monotheism is a moral order with clear resonances with the ideal diagram of the state. A vertical order, integrated with a strong command-and-control structure and compartmentalized into units of worshippers, laws, rules, and codes which descend from the apex. All monotheisms imply sympathy for the pyramid-shaped map of state.

European political theologians in the 18th and 19th centuries saw the ideal of the sovereign state as constructed on the diagrammatic architecture of monotheistic religion. Yet, historically, the dream of monotheism reflects the political forms of its originating era. Despotic states predated the ideal of a despotic god. Vertical political hierarchies are often seen as legacies of religious hierarchies. Here, thinking like a state is tied to an understanding of the European nation as a product of the secularization of early modern religious attachments.[22] Yet monotheism emerges long after the formation of early states. Some early vertically integrated city states offer historical context out of which monotheistic religion arose. A sense of perfect order under a singular hierarchy is embodied in the 'state ideal' of all monotheistic faiths.

Polytheism likewise reflected the networked quality of political governance in Arabia in the early seventh century and the role of city states on the Arabian Peninsula in transitional networks of trade and migration. The challenge to an integrated system of belief and rule was not simply Mohammed's critique of Mecca as corrupt and degenerate. Later Islamists like Sayyid Qutb have similarly critiqued modern liberal capitalist societies.[23] Mohammed's critique was linked to an opposition to the regionally networked model of social life. As Peter Mandeville writes: 'For those who participated in the first migration [the Hijra], then, it was not the geographic move from Mecca to Medina which mattered, but rather the much more dramatic (and initially, one would imagine, disorienting) split from their tribal kin-groups.'[24]

The war between city states which led to Mohammed's victory and pacifying of Arabia gives rise to a problem of succession. Debates around the nature of the resulting early Islamic states are often technical; they centre on how centralized states were, or how similar to European statehood. This highlights the critical role of diffusion in early Islam. A tussle between the horizontal and vertical is the principle dilemma in translating the ummah.

The first caliphs devoted their reign to unifying recalcitrant tribes and expanding territory. But the technical challenges of ruling over such a large territory require a more distributed administration. Tribal identities and affiliations needed to be integrated into ruling methods of order. Centralized administration, especially around familial structures, gave rise to opposition and civil war along the lines of increased factionalism, such as the Khawarij Seceders' failure to acknowledge either Ali or his opponent. The three decades after Mohamed's death witnessed an ambitious state-building exercise. The centre could not hold, and soon rule tipped into a succession of dynasties.

Tensions between demands to unify the territory and tendencies towards diffusing authority are not unique to the history of Islam. The Ummayad dynasty sought to consolidate gains of territory, building a bureaucracy and administration, and extending a period of centralized authority. When their influence expanded to Spain, however, it had to absorb wide cultural diversity, which gradually led to a religious condemnation of the dynastic rulers. They were increasingly perceived as prioritizing politics over religion. The ummah itself begins to take on the character of challenging centralized concentration of imperial power. The idea of a decadent clique of rulers who fail to implement Islam authentically finds its historical roots here. Structured concepts of Islamic law emerged to question the centralizing state. In this early period, founding a real state on the state map of monotheism drove a powerful urge to centralize, while territorial expansion tended towards ever looser control. The centre's desire to control led to accusations of decadence and loss of religious legitimacy. This, in turn, furnished grounds for challenge.

That challenge frequently takes the form of dynastic succession. The Abbasids faced similar centralizing and decentralizing forces. Their capital moved from Damascus to Baghdad, where the new dynasty recognized the higher importance of religious authority. This period is often described as the Golden Age of the Islamic world. Re-Islamization was central to a reinvigorated claim to centralize state power, but it was accompanied by an erosion of political capacity to rule over the sprawling empire. Autonomous local rulers and micro-states emerged. Centralized religious leadership became increasingly nominal. This hollowing out of the state accelerated until the Mongols sacked Baghdad in 1258, by which time the caliph had become a symbolic ruler at most. At this point, the process was reversed. Islam offered a loosening of the vertical dimension; meanwhile, horizontal tensions emerged at the local political level.

Through intersecting centralizing and decentralizing dynamics, a global patchwork of intersecting hierarchical and horizontal relationships was established across the Islamic community of faith. But this was in no sense an integrated state formation along the lines of Europe's state pattern. Thick in its social relations and global, when the unified caliphate disappeared, a cosmopolitan community of traders and social networks emerged, with a vigorous exchange of ideas. Subsequently, a number of distinct Islamic states arose—Safavid, Mughal, and Ottoman empires—each bureaucratically more effective than the last. Tracked by a myriad of globally distributed networks—of Sufi itinerant saints,[25] banking institutions, charitable groups, diasporas, and communities of pilgrims—nested within hierarchies, which in turn nested within networks.

Continuous interaction between centralization and decentralization was inscribed into the historical life of the ummah, just as this marks other global processes today. The ummah is the product of a distinctive assemblage of nomadic and statist tendencies. This too is the history of the world. A globalism built through an interacting push-and-pull between transnational networks and state formations. Nowhere is this more apparent than in recent movements which seek to operationalize the ummah, to build concrete political forms on its ambulant history. Global politics, when not thought of as states, is this process of interaction. Translating the ummah means recognizing global politics as the push-and-pull of networks and hierarchies, with neither dominant.

The Muslim Brotherhood today shows the same vertical and horizontal features that mark out the politics of the ummah. As Alison Pargeter notes, the Brotherhood is difficult to grasp conceptually because it is at the same time a social movement and a political party; it is both transnationally integrated and nationalist; it is Islamist, democratic, pacific, violent, anti-Western, hyper-Western, moderate, and extremist.[26] While most countries in the Islamic world host a branch, each is distinct from the other. Historically, they have provided the main opposition movement in many states. Syria's experience is one of bloody oppression. The Brotherhood binds together a political, financial, grassroots organization with extended European social support and financial networks. The period since 2001 has been fraught with risk for the Brotherhood, and it responded by projecting an attitude of openness and moderation, aligned with various uprisings in the so-called Arab Spring during the second decade of the 21st century.[27]

The Brotherhood, since its founding in Egypt in 1928, has attacked Western modernization as decadent, an attitude embedded in a more widespread anti-colonial story. Its founder, Hassan al-Banna, was part of a reformist movement that viewed a return to the past as promising an uncorrupted future. The movement wove Islamic law into the problem of postcolonial autonomy and uneven development. This movement always contained multiple splits, from which emerged diverse intellectual lines such as the one associated with Sayyid Qutb. Indeed, this particular split has become key to the way people in the West interpret the Brotherhood—its history is described through a contest between moderate, pragmatist liberals and immoderate, traditionalist Qutbists hardened by a history of state oppression.

The expansion of Muslim Brotherhood activities into welfare services, charitable donations, and free clinics for students successfully rooted the group in Egypt's communities. Horizontal structures of social support provided its most effective architectures. Alison Pargeter maps this ebb and flow of political participation as a play of tensions between a reformist current and the traditionalist old guard. Until the mid-1990s, a 'conservative old guard' was in the ascendency within the Brotherhood: any opening was limited by the risk that political engagement with government would result in the loss of the Brotherhood's social base, primarily built on associations with purity. The 'basic contradiction' for the group was between wanting to represent Islam, uncorrupted and pure of politics (the source of its large social base), and the demands of political participation.[28] The Brotherhood is often described as caught between pragmatist politics and its conservative mass support. Carrie Wickham argues that this binary fails to capture the complexity of the movement.[29] There are simply too many different trends within it. Jordanian, Kuwaiti, and Moroccan branches entered formal political participation with significantly differing impacts, and these national contexts created significant breaks within the movement internationally. Partly because of sensitivities, little is known about its international organization, to the point of its existence being denied. When the international organization is talked about, the Brotherhood says it is completely decentralized.[30] Efforts in the 1970s to centralize more hierarchical structures are seen to have been unsuccessful. Given that the movement lacks coherence internationally, it is better understood as 'adaptive' to local circumstances.[31]

Western analyses question whether the Muslim Brotherhood has at times become more or less 'moderate'—that is to say liberal, variously expressed through participation in state democratic processes, openness to rival religious interpretations, tolerance of alternative positions, commitment to rule of law, and Western-style gender equality.[32] Is the Brotherhood a 'normal organization', using Western terms of reference? It is often conceptualized as a movement that experiences tensions at the top between Westernizing, democratizing, or modernizing and traditionalist or dogmatic factions.[33] Where it is questioned in this way, a set of criteria speaks to assumptions of European states and their sense of how politics work.

At stake is the problem of translation. Recoding liberal political concepts into Islamic discourse is not a matter of cross-cultural transmission. Participation in electoral politics has changed the movement in different ways in different places. The evolution of the Brotherhood's rhetoric and behaviour was always local, dependent on branch, personalities, and constituencies. It was mapped onto context but also the needs of external audiences, including European states seeking evidence of liberality. Intersecting complexity, the co-presence of network and hierarchy drove its organizational growth across different states, thus shaping and reshaping its transnational politics.

## Unmapping jihad

Politics of translation can also be seen in attempts to map theologically extreme movements, like al-Qaeda, defined by their acts of violence. Faisal Devji points to the puzzling plethora of sources, aims, sectarian concepts, cultural identities, and appeals, themes, locations, methods, justifications, and arguments that flow through global jihadi discourse. The texts and speeches of leading jihadis show how open the evolution of the global jihad was after 9/11 and how 'pregnant with possibilities' its future remains.[34] In tying a narrative flexibility into its claims to universality, global jihadism constituted, at the time, a uniquely distributed form of militancy.

This was perhaps the most frequently mapped 'terrorist network' in history. Its networked structures were visually represented and re-represented over two decades by states and their intellectual appendages worldwide, who hoped to discover more effective means to its interdiction. The idea that there is a jihadi or extremist story that causes the vulnerable to become more radical or embrace violent extremism should be disrupted; it is a common conclusion of 'extremist network' maps, drawn by counter-radicalization experts. It is argued that these networks introduce interpretations or accounts to relevant populations, and by challenging the narrative-of-self as the backbone of the jihadi virtual community is to attack the will to identify with it and enact terrorist violence. Kinetic responses to jihad are generally seen to be insufficient; attempts by the state to act at the level of ideas is deemed necessary. A battle of ideas has become a popular trope over the last two decades.[35]

This assumption sits in tension with the reality of jihad as a highly networked umbrella which incorporates a bewildering variety of groups and projects.[36] As with the online far right, the global expansion of jihad reveals significant internal differences, not an increasingly solid meta-identity. The emergence of 'home-grown radicals', from domestic populations in Europe in particular, seems to be married to this increasing self-difference of the creed. A paradox emerges for those who represent the jihad as a 'classical' mass mobilization rooted in fundamental identity, since it suggests a direct link between the dynamics of radicalization and storytelling around seeing oneself as different. In 2001, so the argument goes, there may have been something resembling a semi-centralized organization in Afghanistan. But gradually it dissolved into a more decentralized, franchised, and networked organization[37] made up of 'affiliated freelancers'.[38] Proliferation of autonomous groups is explained as a direct consequence of counteraction by security services.[39]

Diffusion spawned a variety of groups espousing differing discourses, political aims, and theological perspectives. Long-documented political division existed between internationalists and religious nationalists.[40] Even among those who agreed the 'far enemy', not the 'near enemy', was the appropriate target of the jihad, there were long-standing divisions over tactics and strategy.[41] Jihadis and Salafis historically entered into a plethora of discussions and disputes, which are by no means linear or easy to categorize.[42] The internet is a battleground between them. Many jihadis share common homelands, historical experiences, and a sense of exclusion in the case of Western diasporas, but this should not be assumed to add up to a global identity.

The radical jihadist community, dispersed across the globe, has limited if any essential characteristics, even if similar threads recur. The jihad draws from narrative flows originating in multiple non-jihadi Islamic subgroups.[43] It is symptomatic of thinking like a state that even in more nuanced works, self-difference is downplayed in readings of their communications. Where difference is acknowledged, it is seen as a weakness in the jihad that might be exploited or as a tendency towards dissolution.[44] Diffusion is seen as a surface phenomenon of the deeper process of forming meta-identity.[45] Consequently, a danger threatens to confuse maps for the territory. Clearly, simplicity makes concepts 'easier to grasp, explain and accept' by tying them into global conspiracy theories and heroic representations.[46] Marc Sageman sees the jihad's strength as being 'all things to all people, who can project their favorite fantasies onto the movement', and while a common denominator is anti-Western political violence, fundamentally 'each group lives in its own world'.[47] Differences inevitably tear movements apart, yet differentiation and decentralization never did lead to implosion, but instead to unfolding growth.

The map of state assumes verticality *is* politics. It is not sufficient to acknowledge the jihad as multiple and plural organizationally. The important point is that the multiplication of jihadi messages, ideas, concepts, motivations, and desires are directly responsible for driving their dissemination. Everything is local here. Having different versions of the same story is neither messy nor disruptive of how to read what drives individuals to embrace violent extremism; it is the discursive dynamic at work. Reproducing jihadis does not come about via linear patterns of mass mobilization appealing to common identity, but through fractal complexity. Political violence grows in multiplying discourses, impacting how people think and, consequently, what they do. The Jihadi movement grows by combining and mutating, thereby absorbing numerous 'heretical traditions'.[48]

Online echo chambers that amplify complexity allow stories to be tapped, channelled, and utilized by local authorities for their own purposes. Online networks are a machine designed to produce novel flows of meaning and storytelling. Hybridized or changed as people add to and spread them, whispers mutate by combining disparate social, political, and cultural desires. The communicators of jihad are pragmatically driven by a desire to unify and to efface differences between groups in their public communications, hopeful of managing the flux of radical viewpoints. However, jihadi movements are not characterized by structural unity, but rather by a series or network of irruptions, clefts, or debates. Precisely this contestation fosters growth by incorporating new struggles, claims, and ideas. The same may now be observed on the Far Right, where diffusion similarly spawns proliferation.

Michel De Certeau concludes 'what the map cuts up, the story cuts across'.[49] No single conductor or narrator dominates the jihad machine, and this renders it 'pregnant', to use Devji's word, with possibilities of all kinds.[50] The jihad grew through a movement built on differences.[51] Herein lies the problem that the map of state poses in the search to understand the future. To think like a state cartographer is always to misunderstand what is happening. But mapping the network can be just as misleading. To make sense of any transnational religious or political movement requires a grasp of how the dynamics of centralization and decentralization intersect, how the vertical and horizontal layer in every historical process to produce meaning and let others shape its interpretation.

**Figure 5.1:** Baltimore and Ohio Railroad, 1840

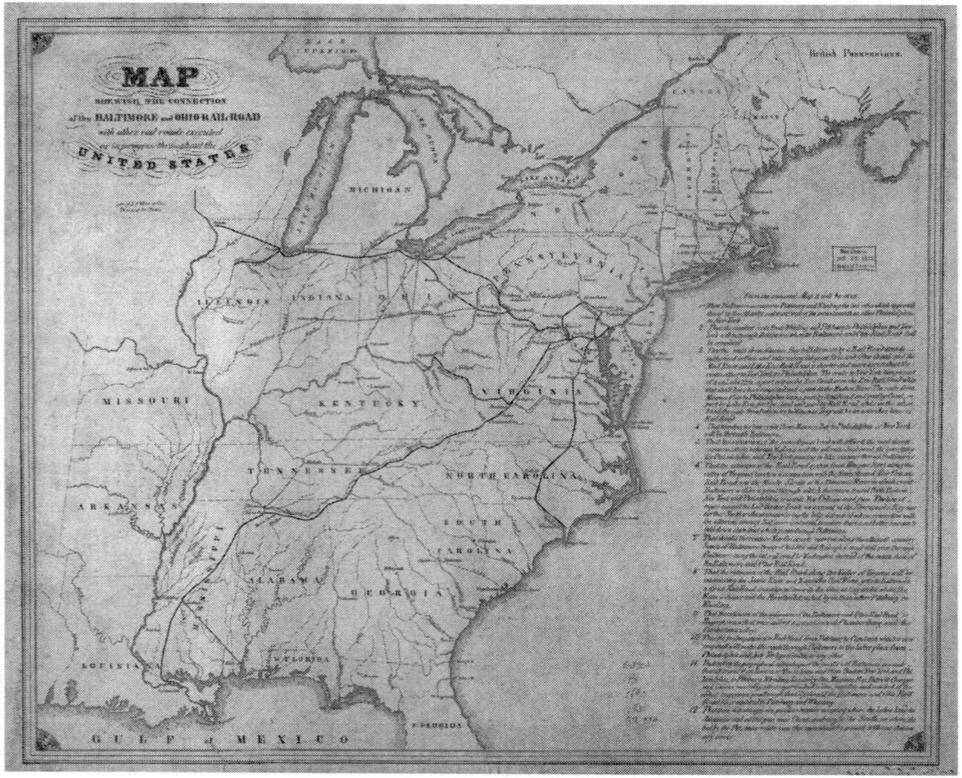


Source: United States Congress National Archive

5

# Bureaucracy and Power

Networks and hierarchies are false opposites. Networks and hierarchies subvert, intersect, and mutually inform both the modern state and its various challengers. Laszlo Barabasi charted the spread of a revolutionary movement called Christianity. He focused not on the charismatic leader, Jesus of Nazareth, but on the Jewish convert Saul, or Paul, as the great proselytizer of a newly formed minority sect. How did Paul transform a minority faith into a worldwide movement that has endured some two thousand years? Barabasi suggests that initially he won approval from the inner circle of power brokers—the disciples of Jesus—to relax the membership rules of the organization, such as male circumcision and strict dietary laws, for anyone wishing to join. Second, he identified how best to spread the word. Paul spent 12 years walking some 10,000 miles between communities, acting as a salesman for the faith. Not just any communities, but the biggest concentrations of population, in which were located the most developed and extensive social networks. These would become the hubs for transmitting the message globally via many links and nodes.[1]

What Paul had identified was a system of cells connected to other cells through different networks. What he carried was what advertising people call a 'sticky' message, one that sticks in the mind of the listener and even makes them want to pass it on to others. As a growing sect that preached monotheism and thus threatened the hegemonic pagan system of worshipping multiple gods, which the Roman Empire cherished, it is not surprising that these social networks should also comprise covert secretive cells. When we speak of networks, we mean hubs which are major nodes or key points of influence. And links are the connections that run between the nodes.

Mark Granovetter established a theory of the impact of friendship networks on the diffusion of information, influence, and mobility opportunity, and community organization. He concluded that it is weak ties, not strong ties, within our networks of friends that best transmit information. One might expect that people we know less well will act as less effective transmitters. In fact, he demonstrates that 'strong ties, breeding local cohesion lead to overall fragmentation'.[2] More inwardly focused strong tie groups, because of their concentrated, uniform character, are less inclined to be linked to other groups. So the message travels less far. Whereas weak ties link to other weak tie groups. Hence transmission of information travels further because these groups are looser and keener to connect with others. Granovetter asked people who had recently changed jobs where they heard of the vacancy. The answer was through people with whom they had marginal or infrequent contact, sometimes from a chance meeting with someone they hadn't seen for many years.

Implicit here is the question of how bureaucratic networks can influence human behaviour by establishing vertical chains that constrain and capture flows of information and other forms of commerce. During the Chinese Zhou dynasty, the military need to draft large numbers of fighters prompted enhanced record-keeping and new logistics. Indeed, Francis Fukuyama argues that: 'the Chinese invented modern bureaucracy, that is, a permanent administrative cadre selected on the basis of ability rather than kinship or patrimonial connection. Bureaucracy emerged unplanned from the chaos of Zhou China (1122–1221 BC), in response to the urgent necessity of extracting taxes to pay for war.' While the early years of the Zhou dynasty were characterized by hierarchical, patrimonial rule through kinsmen appointed within the royal household, palace intrigue was carried out not by individuals, but by an entire family lineage. Consequently, to remove the threat of a coup, a familial lineage in its totality would have to be killed and erased 'to break the rope of descent'.[3] Clearly, this is not very efficient. Thus, new structures arose within the military and what would gradually become the state civil service, which allowed for a broadening of expert participation. And this meant a degree of social mobility within ministerial families of the *shi* social class could arise while aristocrats suffered losses to their numbers in the conflict.[4] These new structures allowed command and control to pass more efficiently through settled chains of relation, which simultaneously restructured social order more broadly, making it more amenable to vertical state mapping.

Likewise, after the probable suicide of Egypt's Queen Cleopatra and the demise of Mark Antony at the hands of Roman general Octavian, who would become the Emperor Augustus, Egypt fell to the control of Rome. So too did its vast grain harvests and revenues that emanated from the rich and fertile Nile Valley. Such was the dramatic effect on the Roman economy from its newly acquired source of grain wealth that the price of bread, a staple of the diet in Rome, fell. Disposable income in the pockets of Romans shot up. More money in the economy forced interest rates on borrowed money to plummet. Low interest rates set off a property boom with citizens looking for a place to invest their new savings. As Peter Frankopan reveals, small teams of tax inspectors were dispatched throughout Egypt with the sole intent of imposing a system of fiscal extraction—a poll tax to be paid by every man between 16 and 60. Following Egypt, the same system was applied to neighbouring Judaea through census-taking and tax collection. That mass population mapping event is captured as a seminal moment in the Christian nativity story. The significance of the birth of Jesus of Nazareth was initially notable for the addition of a future taxpayer on the tax payroll, more than for the purported arrival of a messiah.[5]

By 1 BC, Augustus had begun to eye the celebrated wealth of the Persian Empire. Reconnaissance was undertaken in Axum (modern-day Ethiopia), Sabaea (today's Yemen), and the Gulf of Aqaba. A survey was drawn up of the trade routes that criss-crossed Persia and Central Asia, and the sea lanes that linked the Persian Gulf with the Red Sea. It became a matrix with recorded distances of routes linking the Euphrates and Alexandropolis (Kandahar in today's Afghanistan).[6] This provoked a political revolution inside Persia. A new dynasty, the Sasanians, set about emasculating the power of provincial governors, making them accountable to the central bureaucracy. By using official seals, working practices were rendered more transparent, accountable, and subject to record. The bazaars—public markets—were newly zoned into areas run by guilds, demarcated for producers and traders, where quality and quantity could be better overseen for weights and measures inspection, but ultimately for more accurate and efficient tax collection. Bureaucratic techniques expanded as monies generated new investment into projects such as irrigation, which had the effect of stimulating urban growth and agricultural production. Exports would be catalogued in stamped contracts and stored in official registries.[7]

The rise of vertically integrated bureaucracies like these sits at the heart of the story of modernity. For Max Weber, they represented an ideal type. He did not naively anticipate bureaucracy as a form of selflessness that could remain untainted by ambition and power. Rather, modern bureaucracies were an essential form of organization imported into industrial societies in the late 18th and early 19th centuries. They underpinned the rapid expansion and ever more complex movement of people and goods in the newly created German state after 1871. Bureaucratic integration was central in the new Prussian military and state organization, a paradigm that appeared to draw directly from the mandarin system of administration of imperial China, with its openly contested entry examination and a national to regional to local nested layering of independent, non-patrimonial expertise. Bureaucrats were expected to be professional, independent, objective, meritocratic, and educated, and, thus, highly trained for civil service. Functions would be carefully separated and powers delegated in the form of duties and obligations. But overall control would remain centralized.

These values for managing economic and financial units would soon spread to the corporate sector too. The anthropologist David Graeber observes that 'America's advent as a power on the world stage at the end of the century corresponded to the rise of a distinctly American form: corporate-bureaucratic-capitalism'. This negotiation between forces arose from an economy still dominated by networks of small family firms and high finance. He points to Arrighi's observation that 'an analogous corporate model was emerging at the same time in Germany, and the two countries—the United States and Germany—ended up battling over which would take over from the declining British Empire and establish its own vision for a global economic and political order'.[8]

Yet here too vertical bureaucratic institutions are seen always to be implicated with horizontal network flows. In the 1960s, this was particularly evident in Western universities, where America's and Europe's campuses rang with endorsements of Mao's Cultural Revolution. Institutions otherwise imagined to be conservative by nature and outlook were affected by the counterculture movement. Management schools, in particular, saw the marked influence of Maoist thinking. China's Cultural Revolution would especially be harnessed to re-conceptualize bureaucracy in the West. The management guru Tom Peters set out a manifesto with eight great lessons to reshape and improve performance in capitalist business corporations. These overtly echo Mao's own revolutionary reforms.[9] Yet he also points to the clear organizational advantages in structuring the running of societies hierarchically. When hierarchies mobilize the full spectrum of resources of the state, they can present a persuasive array of cause-and-effect logistics that draw on the strength of industrially marshalled populations, scientifically harnessed science and industry, and focused research and production, and their strategic utility and adaptation in the conflict theatre. Hierarchies take time to mobilize around a common objective, but once set in motion, bureaucratic command and control delivers devastating results by capturing horizontal energy flows, goods, technical skills, and will under a vertically integrated chain.

Only gradually would bureaucracy come to be counterposed to the market in the popular imagination. After all, it had previously formed a key tool in the armoury of the state as it sought to both harness and facilitate the networking flows of capital. As the 20th century unfolded, state agents were increasingly seen to interfere in the free flow of the market. By mid-century, the dominant economic model in many Western states had been some form of Fordist–Keynesian social democracy. As time progressed, 'bureaucracy' would become an increasingly dirty word, associated with bloated and inefficient organizations and an institutional mentality of self-preservation and reluctance for internal reform. Worse still, it would come to represent a totalitarian Big Brother, the expressionless face of state intrusion and official interference into the space of individuals' private lives. Maps, once again, hid from view the complex reality of power's operation through bureaucracies, within but also cutting across different state forms.

## Bonfire of the vanguards

State challengers who confront but also seek to become state actors show the entanglement of vertical bureaucratic institutions with horizontal network flows. Mao in China and Lenin in the USSR—both authoritarian socialists, both believers in central party organization—offer particularly interesting insights into the hierarchy–network dichotomy. These become apparent in their attitude towards the tension between spontaneity and organization; the role of hierarchical command and control; the associated tension between the proletarian mass and peasantry; and a mirror-imaging of the desire to formulate the insurgent challenge through a politico-military architecture that reflects capitalist, industrial, scientific managerialism.

Mao Zedong was the son of prosperous peasants who occupied a more elevated status in the Chinese rural hierarchy. His father would become a grain merchant. His family occupied a higher position in a local hierarchy that comprised eight socio-economic tiers: 'at the top, the big landlords; then small landlords; owner peasants; semi-owner peasants; sharecroppers; poor peasants; farm labourers and rural artisans; and at the bottom, vagrants'.[10] Social relations within the hierarchy committed individuals to accept and respect their place in a structured political economy and within a time-honoured Confucian understanding. According to Peter Zarrow:

> by the sixteenth century villages were linked horizontally and vertically through marketing networks. Generally speaking, a group of villages would each be only a couple hours' walk to a central market that opened perhaps half a day a week (a 'week' being a 10-day cycle). Within this group of villages, people might intermarry, practice the same sets of religious and daily life rituals, speak the same dialect, and seldom leave. ... This was a 'nested hierarchy' of networks each reproduced at a higher level: sets of villages focused on a periodic day market, sets of day markets focused on a market town, sets of market towns focused on a regional center, and so forth. Ultimately this is how the Chinese countryside was tied to international markets.[11]

Mao was a child of rural Hunan. So, he was one of the few Chinese Communist Party (CCP) officials willing to resist the Marxist–Leninist blueprint that Comintern advisers from the neighbouring communist government in the USSR had prescribed for China's workers' revolution. The Soviet model argued for an urban insurgency. The Soviet representatives, after all, could speak from a position of confidence—a platform of success, a world first in revolutionary history secured only three years earlier. Shanghai, however, revealed such ambitions to be misguided on Chinese soil. January 1927 marked a turning point in the fortunes of the CCP as the Chinese

Nationalist Party (Kuomintang—KMT) massacred thousands of communists in China's main economic centre, Shanghai. Meanwhile the KMT held control of most of China's main cities.

For Mao, according to a report he wrote that year, the only viable strategy was to mobilize rural workers and embrace guerrilla warfare—ultimately within what came to be known as his three-phase doctrine of warfare. Steeped in a modernizing philosophy, the CCP would adopt an industrial approach to organizing a politico-military movement in the countryside. Edgar Snow, an American journalist writing during the revolutionary 1930s and 1940s, and among the first to record CCP history and interview Mao and other leaders, had been openly astonished by what he saw.[12] This industrial production, even on a modest scale, sat within a framework of social organization and political decision-making structured in a similar hierarchical manner. And it was the legacy of a coordinated strategy that embraced hierarchical command and control.[13]

The Chinese Communist Party imposed top-down control onto a rural population which itself, over generations, had known nothing other than rigid, hierarchical, nested tiers of networked political economies. Save for the periodic disorder of warlords and military disruption following the demise of the Qing dynastic administration in 1912. The method adopted by Mao's senior command was to mirror a top-down *military* command-and-control structure with a parallel structure of *political* commissars from the national to provincial to local levels. Thus could firm control of the revolution be maintained as a political project achieved through a newly educated mass. The outcome was an integrated synthesis of vertical and horizontal control.

This reflected the logic of Fordism—an economic system of manufacture and social organization that invaded and dominated both public and private spaces in the 20th century. Aldous Huxley's dystopian novel *Brave New World* is set in the year 632 AF (after Ford)—all life is defined by before Ford and after Ford. Indeed, the World State that Huxley conjures up is presided over by a godhead called Ford. His biologically nurtured society is conditioned in every aspect by his industrial principles. But beyond the realms of fiction, the real influence of social and economic engineering would strike a chord in political revolutionaries too. Indeed, 'probably the most committed convert to Fordism', argues Lester Faigley, 'was Lenin, who based Soviet industrialization on the Fordist principles of central planning, hierarchical organization, and large-scale production'.[14]

Henry Ford's automobile factories in Highland Park, Detroit, in 1913 introduced a new system of labour control and production. Large conveyor belts were set up to assemble cars, where discrete tasks were subdivided between workers, each of whom had fixed assignments and distinct responsibilities. Know-how was restricted, acquired only through training passed down by managerial staff. Managers operated within an authoritarian supervisory system that retained a monopoly of control over the plan—the big picture. Hence overall control was centralized and total. The scientific managerial principles of Frederick Taylor would further refine the control over factory time through the application of time and motion studies. He broke down the industrial process into actions during his research in the Bethlehem Steel plant in Pittsburgh. By segmenting parts of the overall process, the time it took to achieve any unit of assignment within the production process could be analysed, accelerated, and made more productive. This Fordist model would become the paradigm for manufacturing around the world for most of the 20th century.

Indeed, it would be embedded within a much greater economic model that tried to impose order on disorder. And that model traded negotiated remuneration and benefits with representatives of labour for greater efficiency and productivity. And profit. Workers received greater material benefits by not striking, therefore producing higher output, and shareholders and management gained greater stability and profits produced from each unit of investment. Even broader, it would sit within a hegemonic consumer–capitalist model that 'sold' objects of desire to an ever better paid workforce. Consumer appetite for cars, home furnishings, and clothes would be encouraged by a persuasive advertising industry and supported by cheap money or credit that offered a utopian lifestyle.

For Vladimir Ilyich Lenin, the discussion revolved around control. To what extent can a mass still dormant in its false consciousness, according to Marxist theory, achieve its revolutionary potential without a vanguard? He says: 'Without the "dozen" of tried and talented leaders (and talented men are not born by hundreds), professionally trained, schooled by long experience and working in perfect harmony, no class in modern society is capable of conducting a determined struggle.'[15] We should not be surprised that both Lenin and Mao, immured in the party machinery of the Bolsheviks and the CCP, should seek to emulate the same administrative, bureaucratic form of the hierarchical states they sought to overthrow and transform. Insurgents and revolutionaries are constrained by the mechanics they can see, for all that they offer a promise of an alternative future. Revolutionary maps seek to show the way to a better tomorrow, but they do so from an understanding of the present which conceals the complex nature of the societal crises from which they hope to escape.[16]

In a rapidly industrializing global marketplace at the turn of the 20th century, Moscow and St Petersburg were home to some of the world's largest manufacturing concerns; larger even than Henry Ford's in Detroit. At the same time, what states had demonstrated during the First World War was an ability to mass-mobilize within a systematic grand plan, turning men into subaltern cogs in the industrial machinery of war manufacture and fighting. When Russian reformists and revolutionaries applied the heady cocktail of Marx's historical materialism and Darwin's evolutionary theories to what they witnessed in the growing urbanization and industrial poverty of St Petersburg and Moscow, they were in effect channelling the workforce into a particular rationale—which offered that workforce a way to harness its dissatisfaction to an overarching narrative of energy and empowerment. Each year, thousands more rural migrants were pouring into the cities, fuelling the industrial workforce and reinforcing social networks of dissenters employed in the iron-making and engineering shops of heavy industrial plant. It is precisely this energy that became the thorny issue dividing political allies.

This leads to the crux of the dispute between political vanguardist Vladimir Lenin and German revolutionary theoretician Rosa Luxemburg—how to manage spontaneous energy, if indeed 'manage' was even the appropriate word? The German activist Luxemburg sought nuance and ambiguity where Lenin favoured simplicity as the prerequisite of victory. Luxemburg valued spontaneity as a fluid and organic force within the population. Lenin regularly flip-flopped in his public statements on the topic, sometimes valuing this supposedly innate source of energy as the starting gun for the revolution, sometimes fearful that the shot, once fired and the force released, could never be brought back under control of the party leadership. For Lenin, consistent with Marxist analysis, the mass needed first to be educated. And that could only be achieved under the guidance of the party leadership. Luxemburg saw this as disrespectful of the masses, squandering their most powerful natural resource. The conduit she advocated was the mass strike, a form of protest that was becoming ever more popular in the early 20th century.

She argues that each situation had to be treated on its own merit. That each revolutionary moment was context specific. Hence the mass strike as a weapon should not be generalized or theorized into irrelevance. She observes:

> It is just as impossible to 'propagate' the mass strike as an abstract means of struggle as it is to propagate the 'revolution'. 'Revolution' like 'mass strike', signifies nothing but an external form of the class struggle, which can have sense and meaning only in connection with definite political situations.[17]

Her language in many ways pre-empts the tone of protest strategists a century on, employing organic metaphors ('adaptability', 'changing', 'opens'—then 'flows', 'billow', 'streams', 'bubbles', 'spring', 'earth') we have come to associate with some later network theorists:

> Its adaptability, its efficiency, the factors of its origin are constantly changing. It suddenly opens new and wide perspectives of the revolution when it appears to have already arrived in a narrow pass and where it is impossible for anyone to reckon upon it with a degree of certainty. It flows now like a broad billow over the whole kingdom,

and now divides into a gigantic network of narrow streams; now it bubbles forth from under the ground like a fresh spring and now it is completely lost under the earth.[18]

This exchange highlights the nature of Lenin as a centralist, an authoritarian, and a believer in the map of state. His successor, Stalin, would usher in decades of bureaucratic socialism that defined the nature and rhythm of the Soviet state. Here there was no substantiation of Friedrich Engels' prediction that following the workers' revolution, the state would one day just wither away. The map increasingly reconstituted the pyramidal territory it represented.

## Network integration

Something else was happening in the late 19th century. A consequence of the rapid expansion of capital was unfolding in tandem with the growth of nation states. In the United States, the dash for the Pacific had become an all-consuming project to define national identity as much as an attempt to dominate territory and bring it under private ownership. Markets would expand hand in hand as scientific advances in modern communications technologies rolled out across the continent. But such was the acceleration in trade and construction, and the success in transporting vast numbers of European immigrants, that the United States found itself face to face with a crisis of logistics. As stock markets fuelled risk-taking and made investment in new railroads attractive, so traffic expanded to fill the newly opened capacity. Official sanction knew few bounds. During the presidency of Abraham Lincoln, the 37th Congress enacted the Pacific Railroad Act in 1862. It allowed the public stock company to build a railroad by cutting through all lands, including those already designated to indigenous tribes. This would provide a further proximate cause to the ongoing Indian Wars which raged between the American state and indigenous people until the 1920s. The Act allowed:

> That the right of way through the public lands be, and the same is hereby, granted to said company for the construction of said railroad and telegraph line; and the right, power, and authority is hereby given to said company to take from the public lands adjacent to the line of said road, earth, stone, timber, and other materials for the construction thereof; said right of way is granted to said railroad to the extent of two hundred feet in width on each side of said railroad where it may pass over the public lands, including all necessary grounds for stations, buildings, workshops, and depots, machine shops, switches, side tracks, turntables, and water stations. The United States shall extinguish as rapidly as may be the Indian titles to all lands falling under the operation of this act and required for the said right of way and grants hereafter made.[19]

A further generous bond issue was made part of the Act; its terms would be even more beneficial to the railroad owners, as it specified the terms of ownership of land where the rail passed through the Rocky Mountains. And an 1864 revision to the 1862 Act would grant extended landownership either side of the track to the railroad companies.

As slavery was banished by the northern states in the American Civil War and Congress routed the new railroad across the north of the country, extensive Chinese labour was attracted as a cheap alternative to work on building the new railroad. Largely drawn from Canton (Guangdong) Province in south-eastern China, workers were imported via a credit-ticket system: their free passage would have to be paid back once they had begun work in the United States. Workers were hired, provisioned, and housed by six Chinese companies in San Francisco, whose identity and origins corresponded to six districts in Canton. The workers came from a network of corresponding villages and clans in China and would later form into their own support groups or secret societies, known as Chinese tongs.

This railroad and others would begin to criss-cross the new nation state with a web or network of communications that wove politics, war-making, and economics together into a national, unified identity. A coalition of business and politics, driven from the eastern cities and Washington, would direct it. Albeit there remained a healthy distrust and tension between private and public ownership in the American body politic.

As the lines fanned out from the east, so telegraph wires were rigged to run alongside rail tracks, connecting fuelling and water depots and stations with information on train passage but also any news of important events. And the demand for news and wish to remain connected with urban centres gave birth to a further network of local, small-town newspapers. Where these minor nodes grew, so too did small towns that both serviced the construction and supply of the expanding network and acted as new homes—new nodes and hubs in a network of occupation and residence—for the hundreds of thousands of migrants that continued to arrive by steamship from Europe, as far afield as the Russian steppes. Railroad companies would be granted up to 10 per cent of the natural land to sell on to migrants, and the state took care of the rest. The network would have to negotiate booms and busts in the stock and commodity markets—that was business. Eventually, haphazard expansion, suffering from an absence of planning and timetables, would lead to a series of crashes in the form of pile-ups involving goods trains on the rail networks.

As James Beniger outlines, this forced into being a 'Control Revolution'.[20] The catalyst for bureaucratic reform would be the train crash on the Western Railroad in October 1841. This railroad handled traffic in the overly congested east coast area. On one stretch of track, opened only the previous day, two passenger trains crashed head-on. Each day, two passenger trains and one goods train were scheduled along the single track, which covered the 156-mile route between Worcester and Albany in New York state. This necessitated nine moments during the day and night when trains would potentially cross. Trains could not wait for each to complete a full journey before the next train had to set off. The procedure meant that one train should move into sidings at a particular point, allowing the other to pass. But in the poor visibility of darkness or fog, head-on meetings were sadly inevitable. The blame for the 1841 crash would be attributed to poor planning and control. And the public outcry was more far-reaching than the loss of two lives. The outcome was to centralize management of the entire Western Railroad into a single headquarters which connected three regional divisional offices in 'solid lines of authority and command'.[21] Each train's working operatives were now issued with bureaucratic rules, procedures, and protocols. Control over engine driver and travelling passengers was vested in the on-board conductor. What was being played out here was a struggle between hierarchy and network.

If the east of the continent had taken two centuries to conquer, the Wild West was brought under control of the new nation state within three decades (the 1860s to the 1890s). But the myth of heroic individualism multiplied by a million homesteaders is quickly undermined by Cameron Blevins, who reveals:

> the real history of the region is one of big government: public land and national parks, farming subsidies and grazing permits, military bases and defense contracts. Arguably no other part of the United States had been so profoundly shaped by the 'state'—a term for the government, institutions, and policies that govern a society.[22]

The author then applies new digital mapping techniques to the emergence of networks in the US postal system. In 1889, Postmaster General John Wanamaker had chronicled 59,000 post offices across 400,000 miles of postal routes. Some 166,000 would eventually be spread across the continent. When seen in context—in 2019, we're informed, 5,362 Walmart stores, 5,472 Wells Fargo bank branches, and 13,914 McDonald's franchises graced the nation—this represents a picture of unstable networks. Characterized as dynamic, ephemeral, and sprawling, digital mapping uncovers how year by year this 'gossamer network' was subject to rapid expansion and contraction.

Overall, what was revealed in the opening up of the continent in the 19th century is how hierarchies and networks are ideal types. Hierarchical bureaucracy was as implicated in network formation as the state was in big business—and as indeed the state form continues to be in the state challenger. Close observation of the symbiotic relationship between order and disorder conjures an image of a mutually defining symbiosis between state and anti-state. Hierarchies contain networks. Networks contain hierarchies, even relatively flat ones. When sales managers from electronics corporations attend trade fairs or when research heads from pharmaceutical companies address academic conferences, they are creating and participating in lateral networks where multiple companies overlap. When those sales managers and research heads return to base and conduct their internal business affairs inside the firm, they meet in groups whose remit cuts across departments; these links too constitute networks. Yet they all exist within conventionally vertical hierarchies.

Those networks which we associate directly with politics, movements such as antiglobalization campaigners, PIRA cells, or al-Qaeda's franchised or platformed organization, retain multiple tiers of leadership—self-selected or elected by some consensual method—which influence or dominate a command-and-control process. What differentiates the political network is a set of features which the anthropologist Luther Gerlach labels SPIN—an acronym referring to its segmented, polycephalous, networked nature. Gerlach researched the counterculture movement across America's student campuses and protest politics of the 1960s. What he observed was the networked development of various social movements, such as Black Power, early feminism, early environmentalism, civil rights, anti-war dissent, and anti-imperialism, or anti-capitalism. He could see how their cells grew, coalesced pragmatically, split, and rejoined when and where necessary. Today, this adaptive thinking about politics is less surprising, conditioned as we have become to descriptions of insurgent movements as both networked and self-generating. Indeed, the network map became increasingly synonymous with counter-state conduct from the 1960s onwards.

All networks are adaptive in an environment replete with various kinds of friction. Networks can 'prevent effective suppression'—multiple leaders can be removed, decapitated in the jargon, and replaced, and the organization will survive. The existence of factions within network organizations increases multi-penetration of ideology when ideas travel along diverse socio-economic cleavages in society. Each cell does its own thing but contributes to the success of the greater whole through duplication, which increases the likelihood of survival—while one cell fails, another survives—strengthening the resilience of the overall system. Networks adapt better to trial and error than vertically integrated bureaucracies. They make mistakes but experiment and innovate. Yet networks can also offer a way of understanding conflict patterns, as

in a network it is a non-linear process involving multiple feedback loops, and the results are often impossible to predict. The consequences of every action within the network spread throughout the entire structure, and any action that furthers a particular goal may have secondary consequences that conflict with that goal.[23]

This new vision of horizontal organization chimed with that of a former ISAF/NATO chief of counter-insurgency in Iraq and Afghanistan, General Stanley McChrystal, when he claimed that it takes a network to fight a network. He talked of 'swapping our sturdy architecture for organic fluidity' as the only way to address the complexity of threats to the state: 'We dissolved the barriers—the walls of our silos and the floors of our hierarchies—that had once made us efficient. We looked at the behavior of our smallest units and found ways to extend them to an organization of thousands spread across three continents.'[24] This is how McChrystal analyses the situation:

> Speed and interdependence had rendered our environment in Iraq incompatible with the vertical and horizontal stratification that had maintained military order for centuries. The distance that carefully regulated information had to travel, and the wickets through which decisions had to pass, made even the most efficient manifestation of our system unacceptably slow. The chains of command that once guaranteed reliability now constrained our pace; the departmental dividers and security clearances that had kept our data safe now inhibited the exchanges we needed to fight an agile enemy; the competitive internal culture that used to keep us vigilant now made us dysfunctional; the rules and limitations that once prevented accidents now prevented creativity. … To beat AQI [al-Qaeda in Iraq], we would have to change into a type of force that the United States had never fielded. … The alternative to our line and block structures had already been developed and tested by Abu Musab al-Zarqawi.[25]

McChrystal captures the problem facing even the most dynamic of military forces. Summing it up as the 'blink problem', he explains: 'A blink was anything that slowed or degraded the process, which often involved a half dozen or more units or agencies working in as many locations. Between each step, information crossed organizational lines, cultural barriers, physical distance, and often time zones.' And quoting one of his briefing officers, ' "By the time we're ready to go after another target," … "it's often days later, the situation has changed, and we're essentially starting from square one." The process felt slow at the time. In retrospect, it was glacial.'[26]

The kind of change needed appeared to exceed the trust-building fundamentals of counter-insurgency practice. A trade-off between securing a threatened population by living among them and, in return, receiving intelligence on enemy fighters was supported intellectually by turning to anthropologists and their 'human terrain teams', who could bring an understanding of the locale and the social networks that criss-crossed it.[27] Find, Fix, Finish, Exploit, Analyse was the mantra. F3EA translated as find the target, watch or fix its movements, send in a force to destroy it, interrogate anyone taken prisoner for their intelligence, and analyse how best to exploit it to undermine its network. To this end, McChrystal introduced a daily summit in an electronic situation room located in Afghanistan but connected to video feeds of experts around the world. By acquiring and processing information through subject specialists in 'real time', informed analysis could be fed back to forces on the ground. Thus were they able to accelerate the flow of knowledge, pre-empt and undermine the enemy's decision-making cycle, and so ultimately change the battle rhythm. The name of the game was speed and acceleration through horizontal deployment.[28]

While Afghanistan witnessed Western militaries with their hierarchical command-and-control structures increasingly embrace a more networked mindset, insurgent fighters of the Taliban—a network of regional and ethnic networks—would eventually move in the opposite direction. At the end of the United States' longest war—a two-decade-long struggle to defeat al-Qaeda and the Taliban—Washington's hasty exodus from Afghanistan in 2021 would heap ignominy and hubris on a failed intervention. Robert Gates had early on asked how the most sophisticated communications nation on earth could be out-communicated by a man in a cave.[29] What would follow would only get worse. Formerly distributed communications among spokesmen representing different Taliban groups began to merge into a centralized voice as the incumbent government's resolve crumbled and resistance melted away in the face of a sudden advance on the capital, Kabul. Within weeks of seizing power, the *Voice of Jihad* (*al-Emara*), for so long the keystone of the Taliban media network, had shifted to become part of state media output. By mid-August 2021, the Bakhtar News Agency and Radio Television Afghanistan had been refashioned. Bakhtar's new head, the erstwhile director of *Voice of Jihad*, Ahmadullah Muttaqi, was now the Information Minister. He would soon become Deputy Director of General Public and Strategic Affairs in the new Office of the Prime Minister. Insurgent broadcasts would subsequently play down ideological content in an attempt to assume the mantle of equitable governance—focusing 'no longer on ideological appeals to its rank and file, potentially more alienating to those who didn't support the Taliban', and instead on 'infrastructure development for foreign diplomacy'.[30] Insurgent networks were rapidly morphing into a state hierarchy.

Hierarchies and networks are deeply implicated, one in the other. Hierarchies contain networks and networks likewise contain hierarchies. As command-and-control cultures and means for imposing order and disorder, they require each other. The map by which we understand the state as the principal ordering mechanism for international life needs to be evaluated accordingly, as does our sense of the 21st century's increasingly violent direction of travel.

**Figure 6.1:** Flock of starlings in the Netherlands

6

# The Battle Swarm

The military drone swarm is currently being advanced as a concept by states including Armenia, China, France, India, Russia, South Africa, Spain, the United Arab Emirates, the United Kingdom, and the United States. Advanced military research programmers share an intuition that the future of warfare is becoming increasingly autonomous, AI driven, and networked. A swarm is more than the sum of its parts. Dynamic feedback allows natural collectives to act in an apparently intelligent manner as a function of individual decision-making and action. Swarms seem to embody a purely horizontal or networked form of organization. No leaders, no hierarchies, no commanding elements to be removed. They are all flow and no verticality.

Gilles Deleuze and Felix Guattari suggest the swarm is the diagram of a pure war machine.[1] In any case, swarms have been of long-standing interest to military planners interested in the value of infesting the enemy and the battlefield.[2] As John Arquilla and David Ronfeldt write in their seminal RAND study,[3] various imitable strategies are associated with swarming in nature, including mobbing, which seeks to overwhelm and confuse an adversary, and pack behaviour, where wolves or hyenas move in small, mobile hunting units, requiring limited hierarchical direction. Military minds hoping to imitate swarms have seen in natural formations a route to more efficient means of killing. Yet the counter-insurgents also worried that they were already too late to the table. Transnational enemies of the state have learned the requisite lessons from the ants, bees, and birds. Swarming belongs to the enemy.

Arquilla and Ronfeldt developed the doctrine of the 'battle swarm' for the US government in 2000. The Global War on Terror would render its arguments increasingly commonplace:

Swarming is seemingly amorphous, but it is a deliberately structured, coordinated, strategic way to strike from all directions, by means of a sustainable pulsing of force and/or fire, close-in as well as from stand-off positions. It will work best—perhaps it will only work—if it is designed mainly around the deployment of myriad, small, dispersed, networked maneuver units.[4]

Drawing lessons from the natural world as well as from the history of war, they suggest that imitating the swarm has often proven 'a very effective way of fighting'—so effective, they suggest, that this kind of strategic formation may become the future model of war, centred on 'well-informed, deadly small units'.[5] Such mobile units were already the modus operandi of the most inventive state challengers to have emerged from the paradigm shifts of the 1990s. Ethnonationalist paramilitaries, right-wing lone wolves, home-grown jihadis, and rite-of-passage salafis are lumped together with civil society actors, autonomous media communicators, and antiglobalization protestors.

New technologies, they argue, have for the first time rendered the swarm and infestation a viable strategic model for militaries. At the turn of the millennium it seemed clear that: 'Whoever masters this form will accrue advantages of a substantial nature. Yet, networking alone is not enough; just organizing into a network is no guarantee of success. There must also be principles and practices—a doctrine—to guide what a networked force should do and how it should behave.' If a militarized network is the form, the swarm is the doctrine 'for networked forces to wage information-age conflict'. The technology may be widespread, but 'moving toward swarming is going to be more a function of cultivating an appropriate turn of mind and a supple, networked military form of organization than it will be a search for new technologies'.[6] A way of seeing was at stake, gearing the map to more effective strategic action on the battlefield.[7]

In search of this new strategic turn of mind within the history of war, an evolutionary trend towards swarming emerged, from the melee to massing to manoeuvre to swarm at the end of history.[8] Each military formation overlaps and builds on the experience of the last. A classical step theory of history is in evidence here. What changes, however, between each stage is how information flows through the organism of the military body. The map of history implies an uninterrupted flow of information as the end point or telos. Melees require the least information flow; a riot requires no communication. Massing requires single directional information. Manoeuver requires more information, but movement remains unidirectional, weighing where force should be applied and shifting as a campaign progresses. Swarming requires sustained and systematic communication from each point to each point in real time. As ants leave pheromone trails, bees 'dance' patterns of movement, and starlings imitate each other, in each, information flows from individual to individual—there is no central or mediating node. Information moves freely. Arquilla and Ronfeldt's claim is that swarming is best practised by terrorists, criminals, fanatical groups, and civil society non-governmental organizations (NGOs), which proliferated in the second half of the 20th century. The state must consequently evolve towards a break with its own logic of verticality.

Arquilla and Ronfeldt's was a call for a new strategic map. If the state hoped to survive, it would need to adapt the map of its enemies. The state must learn to fight like a network: to infest its enemies, just as their enemy infests the state. It could do so because, they argue, the swarm is not a counterpoint to the state. The swarm is not the essence of revolution. Revolutions since the early 20th century relied no less on connecting vertically structured social movements that could hold mass demonstrations against colonial empires, only to create, all too often, authoritarian or theocratic regimes. Arquilla and Ronfeldt argue that even the best cases of 'social maneuver',[9] like Gandhi's non-violent campaign to undermine British rule in India, employed general strikes and protest that involved 'swarming' tactically, but only in a traditional hierarchical strategy to overthrow the state. A general strike cannot adequately capture and remobilize that state. It can only provide a step in that process.[10]

According to Rosa Luxemburg, riotous horizontal effects give anti-state actions their unpredictable potency and creative dimension.[11] Revolutionary movements must find some balance between spontaneity and the need for organization. And this is why they so often slip into authoritarian politics or excessive violence (or indeed both together). Each revolutionary movement is balanced between directive vertical organization, according to Leninist vanguardism or managerialism, and an explosive horizontalism. Hence Arendt's implication, that the revolutionary harnesses forces that are not of the state in order to capture the state, is appropriate.[12] This raises the question of what sits at the heart of the revolutionary dynamic. The tactic of the general strike, if understood as a function of an alternative diagram pitted against the state, suggests the essence of revolution is the swarm: a disruptive flow prior to the managerialism that makes use of it. In revolutionary thought, then, we see the politics of a map different to the state's: the swarm as abstract map of another politics—a condition of possibility and perhaps deepest tendency.

How could swarming be adopted by militaries? The RAND study was implicitly defensive, proposing 'wholly new thinking' to avoid being left behind by decentralized opponents. Yet this leads to contradiction. State swarming requires integrated surveillance and communications systems. To achieve complex, multilevel attacks—the 'signature' of a swarm, with 'sustainable pulsing' of forces and/or their fire—independent units must connect as a fluid network.

When the state networks its military in this way, a problem arises rooted in the need to make the members of a swarm communicate effectively across the entire body. In Alexander Galloway's view of the map of the 'distributed network', all the nodes must 'speak the same language' if they are to function.[13] The technical problem is that interconnectivity needs shared standards or common protocols. Were a swarming army to lose control of those protocols, it could not act coherently in pursuit of strategic ends of the state and its relationship to political governance. To balance adaptability and control as tools of statecraft, they must use communications technologies that are inherently vulnerable to interdiction. A state swarm needs uninterrupted flows of information across the network. Any jamming of information sends the swarm back to disorder. Consequently, Arquilla and Ronfeldt call for an informational network to cover the entire swarm. 'Robust communications that help with both the structuring and processing of information will enable most pods and clusters to engage the enemy most of the time' in an organized fashion.[14] Yet this call is antithetical to the swarm. The need to communicate across entire networks contradicts the logic of the swarm—where all communication is proximate from local actor to local actor. The vulnerability they anticipate assumes a criterion for success that is rooted in the map of the state.

In thinking like a state, the military struggles to swarm. In the dream of the state swarm, something is timeless. It is self-directing; it can learn and grow without input from the centre. When military minds worry that their communications across the swarm might be interrupted, they reveal the long shadow cast by the state map. Revolutionaries face the inverse problem

## Safety nets

In the first decades of the 21st century, military planners turned their attention to threats emerging within their own states. Specific communities were marked out as containers of risk and uncertainty by incorporating online and offline networks that threatened to grow into violence. How to reach into these communities became an urgent challenge for states who wished to pre-empt these network effects and their potential militarization. Paul Virilio had predicted the way in which war becomes domesticated over time as logics of military organization enter into politics through informational conflict and the rise of network actors.[15] He anticipated the emergence of societies that would be more or less explicitly administered by military thought. He predicted a final blurring of the lines in Clausewitz's triad (State–Society–Military), where the division between states, their societies, and their militaries would collapse as a function of necessity. The return of military thought processes to the home front in response to global insurgency and hybrid war brings about profound uncertainty—this is a battlefield where the state believes itself to be the least well adapted operator.

At the root of this belief is the sense that networked organizations, whether al-Qaeda or Al-Shabaab, Extinction Rebellion or Black Lives Matter, function because their modus operandi relies on tapping into pre-existing sources of horizontal cohesion within society. These may be clan and religious identifications, family ties, or groundswells of community activism. Horizontal qualities allow them to subsist in the face of overwhelming force from the state. Remove a 'key node' with an arrest or drone strike and it has little effect: worse, it catalyses reproduction. Network actors from the Taliban to Génération Identitaire to QAnon extract this elastic function from pre-existing societal milieus. Every state action to interdict these groups runs the risk of accelerating their growth by feeding their distributed network. Every setback leads to later resurgence.

How to address these concerns? 'Resilience thinking' has entered the military and increasingly shapes its politics. It attempts to inoculate a system from fatal damage by enhancing its ability to withstand and recover from any crisis. Encouraging resilience, whether in a critical infrastructure, a community facing economic or social stresses, or an ecology affected by climate change, is a way of folding future risk into the body in question. That way, its openness to the unexpected becomes a source of productivity: people will benefit from adapting. The more resilient, the better able they will be to learn from negative external stresses. Unsurprisingly, governments worldwide are investing significantly to promote greater resilience across societies, at home and abroad, to all manner of threats, existential anxieties, and insecurities.

The swarm understands resilience because adaptability is the defining quality of any horizontally networked formation. That is also why it attracts states. The persistence of networks, when faced with uncertainty, frustrates command-and-control structures but also seduces them. Resilience requires a form of thinking that is neither causal nor predictive, but precautionary and anticipatory. Likewise, to swarm is to set aside any hope of controlling events, instead expecting flux and fluidity in conditions of innovation and surprise. Resilience thinking runs on a logic opposed to that of the state map. It can be used by the state, but only by reconceiving what the state is in relation to its society.

David Chandler suggests that early iterations of 'resilience' have tipped into a desire to look for entangled complexity in everyday life. As people gaze into these complex depths, the 'intractable nature of the problems addressed, their failure to be captured by external "problem-solving" ... forces policy-makers to see the nature of the interactions and connectivities which construct the world itself'. This pushes beyond the capabilities of mapping, since 'no matter how much external actors attempt to "drill down" to the specificities of the context it seems they will never grasp the infinite complexity of causation and emergence'. The unmappabilty of the world's natural 'depths' is revealed by the dream of resilience.[16] Terror, for the state at least, is one inevitable consequence. The 21st century is read as the century of networked threats running across society; they tie together pandemics, migration, economic shocks, climate change, terrorism, and decaying social cohesion. The challenge faced by states, then, is how to think horizontally while remaining in command of events. In other words, to design for permanent crisis. Resilience thinking, just like strategic swarming, requires unmapping the state itself.

The origins of resilience thinking reside in ecological debates about efficient resource management. Resilience thinking emphasizes

> destabilisation of the notion of 'equilibrium' as the core of the ecosystem concept and the normal terminus of ecosystem trajectory, and the beginning of a major shift among ecologists away from the notion that there exists a 'balance of nature' to which life will return eventually if left to self-repair.[17]

The central observation of its leading advocate, Holling, is that when responding to pressures, ecologies evolve. But there is a level at which this can no longer be effected. Ecological time is not linear, slow, or incremental. It proceeds in sudden jumps and breaks, which may prove catastrophic in their consequences for ecosystems.[18] In the 1990s, Holling founded the consortium of environmental scientists called the Resilience Alliance. More recently, these initiatives have been brought together within the Stockholm Resilience Centre, a high-profile think-tank which promotes the uses of resilience theory in international environment and development projects. Resilience concerns the point, within any system, at which a shift to a new balance is imminent. This may be a permanent change to the ecological balance of populations within an ecosystem (more jellyfish in the seas, perhaps) or a new Ice Age. In resource management, if a bureaucracy pays insufficient attention to boundary criteria, a desert-like new normal can rapidly emerge. Ecological and political systems are interrelated in feedback loops. 'Entanglements' sit at the heart of all potentially catastrophic environmental or societal transformations.[19]

The concept of resilience only aligns with the state map when two questions are asked: What allows me to continue in a recognizable form? How much change can I absorb before I am no longer recognizable? Resilience thinking has been applied to thinking about individual responses to trauma, acknowledging breaking points but also how identity is sustained through evolution. Every person is the product of a lengthy negotiation with social, economic, and cultural forces it wants to capture under its own vertical diagram. This is the same challenge facing the state. The state has always been in a permanent condition of contestation with complex networks that make it up. This is why no state looks like its map.

Building resilience is an increasingly popular approach to anticipating emergencies, seeking to tackle future threats through capacity building.[20] Structures of command and control *must* break down in the face of unexpected disruption. Just as the internet, with its protocols of decentralization, was 'designed as a solution to the vulnerability of the militaries centralised system of command and control' against the challenge of nuclear war. Resilience is fundamentally about embracing redundancy as a characteristic of self.[21] This is why the state cannot and never has mirrored its vertical diagram. The more centralized the network, the more vulnerable it is to shock. The more distributed the network, the more redundancy is built in and the more securely it functions. Where does the state derive its resilience? From below. In search of resilience, the state does not construct more levees; it builds the capacity for precarious communities to self-organize in moments of crisis, to help each other—by moving another's car away from rising floodwaters.[22] To borrow from Anna Tsing, we see how the process of breaking down is implicated in the construction of new societal forms.[23]

Seeking community resilience has an extensive presence in literatures on counter-terrorism and counter-insurgency but also post-conflict reconstruction—how fragile community relations are restored following conflict by reinforcing existing nets of local solidarity. Resilience thinking focuses on how horizontal formations have an inherent stability or robustness to shocks which, if harnessed, can aid reconstruction. This may appear as local knowledge or as key community actors who perform as negotiators in traditional societies.

Distributed structures of social solidarity in Afghanistan have never aligned with central government. Which explains the hubris of foreign campaigns to reinforce it. Attempts to bypass local authority structures are never successful. Where structures are weakened by civil war, they often remain the only ones functioning. What makes society resilient is rarely what the West imagines as essential civil society structures, made up of activist or rights groups, unions, or churches. When imported, these do little to erode the resilience of longer-standing conservative societal networks.

Where a state is not aligned with the map, state failure occurs. Yet resilience of an entity like the Taliban is rooted in a deep synergy between horizontal and vertical structures in societies that constitute Afghanistan. The state map may not be visible. But these are nonetheless resilient structures which are more effective than the central government has ever been. Resilience is no panacea for the state and its military objectives. Resilience reflects a different map, which the state map struggles to incorporate and often works against.

Authors who write on resilience recognize that cities are particularly complex and interdependent systems, vulnerable to a variety of threats, both natural and human. An emphasis on the networked quality of the urban environment appears in discussions around transportation and critical infrastructures. Significantly, choke points permeate all networks, leading to risks to chains of communication and passage. These choke points could be power stations, water purification plants, internet nodes, banks, or bridges. What allows flows of money, people, goods, or ideas to move through society is critical. The global coronavirus pandemic has illustrated this. Global supply networks mirror local and international vectors through which viruses spread, as well as mutate. These are in turn mirrored by vaccine hoarding. States want to capture the networks they sit astride. They wish to reassert their own lines by asserting command over these new flows.

Securing critical infrastructure in states and their urban centres is big business. And it is set to increase in the coming decades. It does not simply protect sites, but builds sufficient redundancies into societies. Since the 1980s, a central feature of states' economic doctrine has been to distrust 'perfect knowledge and an epistemology of limited foresight. The complete predictability of future states of the world is, for them, not only an empirical, but also a logical, impossibility'. This underpins the 'intuitive ideological fit' between resilience and contemporary capitalist societies.[24]

The rise of resilience thinking is mirrored in the growth of societies in the West, read as the story of a uniquely liberal state. For some commentators, the spread of resilient logics across multiple fields of thought is responsible for populations accepting new patterns of precarity in individuals' lives—something liberal societies had chosen not to accept in the past.[25] As a consequence, resilience is seen as pointing beyond the liberal state to new horizons of darkening political order.[26] Resilience-building policies and practices are often criticized for failing to ensure people have space to act and build the kind of states and polities they want. Promoting resilience cannot be a matter of politics, in this account because it encourages people to accept existing structural conditions rather than change them.[27] To become resilient to climate change risks failing to prevent polluting, for example. Or, if social democratic states are to be made resilient to the pressures of global capital flows, they must become nimbler and more competitive. They will need to scale back their social safety net for the sake of long-term economic adaptation and competitiveness.[28] These critiques may miss the point. Resilience understood as state swarming is rooted in understanding that value can be gleaned from uncertainty. Hence it echoes Schumpeter's ideal of creative destruction in the marketplace; the chance of being outcompeted encourages greater efficiencies in bureaucratic management. Here, a vertical map seeks to integrate the horizontal within it.

The swarming logic of redundancy at the centre of resilience thinking reflects an unmapping which has always been co-present with and co-constitutive of the state. Resilience is not new. Resilience thinking marks the triumph of an archaism, rediscovering swarming horizontal cartographies that were always at the root of state formation. The possibilities of the resilient swarm were visible from the ancient states of Mesopotamia. Swarming nomadic armies were, after all, what the first urban despots had to hold back if they were to retain power. The diagram of the resilient swarm promises new possibilities for modern politics, as does the diagram of the vertically integrated state pyramid. Politics is what happens between these maps when they interact.

We have always lived in swarming states. Today's networking of the state is tied to a sense that we cannot control or predict urban life perfectly, that we have to accept conditions of complexity.[29] Modern cities, as Benjamin Bratton notes, are smart 'megastructures' designed around algorithms to predict the future.[30] Resilience thinking embodies the state's attempt to think using the network map, dropping the ideal of command and control so as to distribute decision-making down the chain. All states in history have attempted to manage swarms living within them. Vertically organized politics has tried to think horizontally, to take into account complexity and uncertainty. To mitigate top-down planning, controls, thinking, and organization; to avoid a control room holding all information, synthesizing it, and deciding the best course of action. Unsurprisingly, states' attempts in this area have proven problematic and prone to reversal. States who try to 'do resilience' or 'think like a swarm' are caught in a bind. At stake is a contradiction between two maps. Each map contains different accounts of how things work. To live with uncertainty and introduce organizational forms to cope with counter-state threats that swarm, including climatic or virological events, demands an unmapping of the state.

## Revolution and persistence

The need for permanent negotiation between verticality and horizontality is clear when state challengers explicitly adopt a strategy of resilient swarming. *Foco* was a theory of state challenge most closely associated with the Cuban Revolution. Developed in the theoretical writings of Ernesto 'Che' Guevara and Régis Debray, it was a post facto, if not romanticized, rationale of events leading up to the Cuban Revolution in 1959. This adaptation of Mao's three-stage warfare model of revolution saw the urban environment as a tactical realm where actions are taken only to support strategic actions in the countryside. First to encircle, then, at the final stage of the revolutionary process, to capture towns as the seats of political authority. In the city the state is too strong, so its enemies need to find other spaces.

This strategic map prioritizes guerrilla nomadism in the early stages of any struggle against the state. It avoids creating settled zones of territory that insurgents might need to defend, at least until their force is strengthened. This reflects something akin to resilient swarming. Small groups in the countryside swarm until they can coalesce into a larger army to take the cities. The strategic case bears the hallmarks of later resilience thinking. Emphasizing the capacity to bounce back from failure, extreme mobility, decentralization, and tactical adaptability in the face of losses. Early settlement by revolutionaries into organized enclaves invited losses in terms of troops, equipment, and symbolic capital.

Régis Debray argues that holding independent revolutionary safe havens, as utilized by Mao, had shown insufficient resilience to attacks from more organized and better resourced state forces.[31] Resilience thinking runs through his *Revolution in the Revolution?*, where he critiques sedentary strategy for failing to be flexible and learn from past mistakes. Fidel Castro had learned from Simón Bolívar 'tenacity' in the face of defeat. Tenacity should be the lesson of a Cuban revolution, to survive 'false starts and so many errors'.[32] The new strategic orientation should assume that 'for a revolutionary, failure is a springboard. As a source of theory, it is richer than victory: it accumulates experience and knowledge.'[33] Debray's book is suffused with an injunction to recognize how preexisting revolutionary maps failed, and to learn from them.

This mirrors Guevara's argument that the positive quality of a guerrilla is an attitude of 'not being dismayed at any time' and persevering to learn.[34] Both authors agree: the state enemy has a disciplined professional army and bureaucracy and so can resist any damage inflicted by revolutionary forces. In the early stages, the guerrilla army, by contrast, has little capacity to suffer damage. Its limited arms supplies mean that every lost gun is one loss too many. The guerrilla must retrieve any weapons from fallen comrades. Their limited numbers mean every fallen comrade is a catastrophe. Where every 'enemy loss is always repairable', to repair a guerrilla unit takes time and effort.[35] When the guerrilla force is young, it is particularly vulnerable to obliteration from a frontal attack. To maximize their ability to prolong the struggle, insurgents swarm to survive.

The guerrilla movement begins by restricting its actions to limited hit-and-run attacks. Consequently, at an early stage, the struggle takes on a 'negative quality, an attitude of retreat'.[36] So a necessary characteristic of guerrilla struggle is mobility. Guerrillas must constantly flee encirclement, luring the enemy into traps, retreating to attack from different points continuously, and making the most of the cover of darkness. Because losses are never equal between guerrilla and enemy, towns and cities must be avoided. In the city, it is too easy to be encircled. Engaging in urban and suburban warfare means fighting on the least favourable ground for rural guerrillas. Groups must be smaller to survive, since they cannot venture far from the area where they operate. Speed of withdrawal must overcome any distance on the ground. Near to or in cities, *foco* operates best at night; encirclement will probably lead to death.[37]

The fundamental characteristic of the guerrilla is flexibility, the ability to adapt to circumstances: 'Against the rigidity of classical methods of fighting, the guerrilla fighter invents his own tactics at every minute of fight and constantly surprises the enemy.'[38] For success, the guerrilla takes 'only elastic positions, specific places the enemy cannot pass, and places of diverting him'. The guerrilla's 'form of attack ... start[s] with surprise and fury, irresistible ... [and] suddenly converts itself to total passivity', allowing the enemy to relax and then striking again.[39] Only a combination of surprise and rapidity allows guerrillas to balance the greater resilience of their foe. Nomadic ability to retreat and escape encirclement with tactical flexibility represents a strategy of resilience turned against the state.

To be intimate with the environment is critical to achieving network power. Radical nomadism in the early stages of revolution requires selecting the most favourable ground, such as mountains or swamps, which still allows lines of communication to be kept open. The more unfavourable the ground, the greater their mobility and speed relative to the enemy, and the smaller the revolutionary group must be. Fighting on open plains renders them vulnerable to encirclement. Debray is explicit: at the nomadic early stages, the only advantage a guerrilla force has over an army is mobility and flexibility. The aim is to disperse an enemy's expeditionary force in the countryside, reduce its maoeuvrability, ensure its rear guard is never secure.[40] To scatter and continually attack and weaken its elite forces. It is critical to deny the 'idea of unassailability'—in other words, not assume the enemy army is resilient—while degrading its morale. Debray recognizes that *'guerrilla forces are weak everywhere and the enemy, however scattered he may be, is strong everywhere'*. The enemy will seek always to destroy the *foco* in the early stages 'without giving it time to adapt itself to the terrain or link itself closely with the local population or acquire a minimum of experience'.[41]

Guevara argues that guerrillas had to seek out inaccessible positions and only then 'proceed to the gradual weakening of the enemy', moving incrementally deeper into enemy territory and wearing the state down through its greater harmony with the environment. Guerrillas depend on the support of rural populations, whose knowledge of the countryside allows them to hide. Only intimate knowledge of the environment allows them to combat the superior strength of the enemy. Rural strategy is one of exhaustion: 'blows should be continuous', aiming to deprive the enemy of sleep and attack morale by giving them the impression of being surrounded.[42] Through sabotage and organizing strikes, 'it is possible to paralyze whole armies', suspend industrial life in an area, and leave the city without factories, light, water, communications and their people unable to travel at night. As 'the morale of [the enemy's] combatant units weakens ... the fruit ripens for plucking'.[43] Guerrillas must act like a swarm, a natural force eating away at the resolve of the enemy and gradually eroding the state.[44]

Benefits of rural swarming are framed as resilience. For Guevara, it entails developing the right character. The hard life of guerrillas in the countryside encourages character building, a process that symbolizes the wider struggle. Much is made of the guerrilla's willingness to suffer: 'staying in the wildest zones, knowing hunger, at times thirst, cold, heat, sweating during continuous marches, letting the sweat dry on his body and adding to it new sweat without any possibility of regular cleanliness'. All are essential to the guerrilla spirit. Individuals must train to suffer 'formidable privations', to live in the open air, to suffer inclement weather.[45]

> All possible precautions ought to be taken to avoid a defeat or annihilation. ... [T]o survive in the midst of these conditions of life and enemy action, the guerrilla fighter must have a degree of adaptability that will permit him to identify himself with the environment in which he lives, to become part of it, and to take advantage of it as his ally to the maximum possible extent [using] adaptability and inventiveness.[46]

The movement must progress from small to large, from one to many: the 'small motor sets the big motor of the masses in motion'. A long period of nomadism is necessary because the *foco* needs time to grow until it has acquired the character and resilience of a regular army, capable of dealing the final blow to defeat the enemy. The key point, however, is that swarming is only successful in the preliminary stage. Only a hierarchical leadership can innovate and develop strategies to capture the state. Pragmatically, a unified leadership is necessary to prevent overzealous decentralization. It is critical, Debray believes, that the 'concentration of resources and men in a single *foco* permit the elaboration of a single military doctrine, in the heat of the combats in which men receive their training'.[47] Should swarming be taken too far, capturing the state becomes impossible.

With a concern for adaptability, flexibility, and mobility comes the need to learn from failure, to bounce back stronger with an improved plan. Guevara and Debray were strategists of resilience against the state. But they are only partial advocates of horizontal swarming. They correctly saw in the swarm a politics that could not be reconciled with capturing the state or with resolving any form of governance. For governance, hybrid forms bring swarming together with vertical command and control. *Foco* partially adopted the naturalistic logic of resilience. But its practitioners intended to capture the verticality of the state and apply it to new functions.

Swarms eat what they find. Herein lies the secret of Islamic State and its short-lived territorial dominance in Syria, where the oscillation between crushing verticality and explosive power of horizontalism dictated the violent trajectory of its history. Here too are the underlying mechanics of the online Far Right, which embraces strategic swarming, and the seeds of its emergent catastrophism. They take the form of an acceleration into an inevitable race war.[48]

**Figure 7.1:** Circuit board

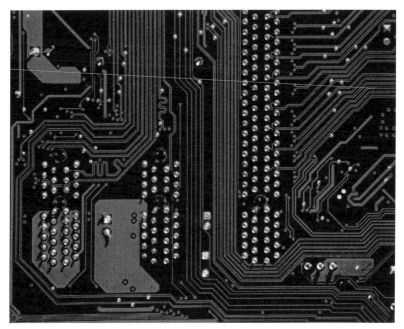

Source: Unsplash; photo by Michael Dziedzic

7

# Information and the State

To make sense of the world, tools are needed to turn data into knowledge. Data are raw, unprocessed, before being observed and collected; information is data processed through a cognitive map; knowledge is information enriched with reflection on the cognitive map. In today's digital information space, the simplistic idea of there being only senders and receivers, producers and consumers, has given way to a world where receivers are simultaneously producers of knowledge. Everyone has become a communicator. This has further entrenched the binary between vertical and horizontal cognitive maps. Everyone has become their own cartographer now. Against the free flow of information across digital networks of communication runs a counter-drive to control information flows. Regulated processes set out to contain and standardize what value—and value is a form of meaning—is attached to freely flowing commodities.

Weights and measures was a principle of audit introduced into emerging modern economies five hundred years ago. Although its precursors are to be found in markets and bazaars dating back thousands of years, where goods were bartered through approximations of value attached by buyer and seller. Methods for weighing goods or measuring dimensions would come to carry the state seal of approval, enforced by independent auditors or verifiers and ultimately backed by the legal system. This meant that trade could be harmonized, disagreement avoided, and exchange sped up. The more friction could be extracted from society, the easier it was to regulate behaviour into predictable patterns and outcomes.

*Homo communicator* is a creature of standardization. Every person sits at the heart of moving volumes of traffic around systems. But carriers of goods or routes along which carriers travel with their goods demand with increasing urgency that movement be freed up, sped up. Different routes and connecting networks should endure less friction and fewer delays. Consequently, any need to transfer, translate, or renegotiate onward passage threaten that ambition. To accelerate movement is to reduce friction or resistance.

Standardization reconfigures the shape of what is being shifted. Goods are boxed to standard dimensions, loaded into standard-sized containers, and rolled on and rolled off trucking fleets and container ships that ply networks of trade routes across the world's oceans. Rectangular boxes of uniform dimensions make for faster transfer and more efficient storage than an assortment of oddly sized packages. Containerization has changed our lives in the consumer age. It has changed the way states engage with global markets too.

For most readers, to talk of information is to conjure up the image of characters and numbers on a page or screen. To see the shipping of consumer goods, oil and gas supplies, and raw materials and foodstuffs as information rather than consumables requires a little more imagination. However, states and state-regulated corporations, particularly in bureaucratic nation states, increasingly seek to reduce all transfers and exchanges to packages of numerical data. Numbers tell stories.

A direct genealogy connects the emergence of weights and measures, minting of coins, accounting and double-entry bookkeeping to regulated audit of businesses with technologies of information capture. The common denominator? Standardization. While the abacus was an early technology for calculation, it was also a way of capturing data that gave the user greater control over the trading environment and an advantage over competitors.[1] Published in Venice in 1494, 27 pages of Fra Luca Pacioli's *Summa de Arithmetica, Geometria, Proportioni et Proportionalita* deal with accounting— 'Particularis de Computis et Scripturis'. 'In the High Middle Ages, thanks to a revival of trade, the development of companies and their growth in complexity, the double-entry method was invented.'[2] Hand in hand, it accompanied the development of Hindu–Arabic mathematics: 'The manner in which mathematics developed in Renaissance Italy owed much to the commercial revolution following the crusades and the resulting expansion of trade and the establishment of a system of agencies distant from the center of the business and long-term partnerships than one-off business ventures between two people.'[3] However, a century before, it is believed, the double-entry system was already in use in the merchant houses of Venice, Tuscany, Genoa, and Milan with their expanding workforces and trading relations in foreign countries beyond their immediate surveillance.[4]

Similarly, the Microsoft Excel spreadsheet with its programmable calculating capacity seeks to contain information, to manage it, before distributing it in systems and patterns recognizable to hundreds of millions of users in the world today. Apple founder Steve Jobs would later celebrate the spreadsheet, saying: 'there have been two real explosions that have propelled the industry forward. The first one really happened in 1977 and it was the spreadsheet.'[5] Since its commercial appearance as Excel 1.0 on 30 September 1985, the spreadsheet software within Microsoft Office has been taken up by one in every fifth person on the planet.[6]

Information should not be random, nor stand outside agreed conceptual frameworks. That it can be more easily connected to state regulators in digital form, replacing the slower, more cumbersome paper records of only a generation ago, is less significant than its role as a tool of discipline and punishment. Compulsory audits of company accounts using standard methodologies—a verification technology to screen erroneous balance sheets—emerged in the years preceding the outbreak of the First World War. A trade union movement was wary of throwing its weight behind the struggle between competing imperial powers—in effect, committing its members to fight fellow workers in the international brotherhood of labour—and it exacted a price for its commitment. Beyond improvements to employment benefits, won for their members from a government in need of manpower and firepower, they engineered a situation where profiteer capitalists, who stood to make fortunes from the war effort, could no longer operate with impunity. Money flows could be surveilled through a unified set of auditing criteria and carried out by state-accredited professionals. More broadly, Michael Power observes that:

> Audit demands something standardizable to audit. … In the audit society everyone knows about the crudity of such measures, but the imperative of auditability overrides these doubts and qualifications, such is its irresistible logic. Thus not only do audits create and reinforce conditions for their own functioning, but they seek to do so by creating a new bureaucratic 'surface' or social reality which is highly standardized.[7]

The Fordist model of industrial production aimed to segment the chain of manufacture into specialized standard units of work that make for more efficient control of time and space. Labour and materials are equally commoditized and share a common accounting base. Standardization makes for more easily regulated bureaucratic or managerial processes too. Standard protocols and default practices mean that organizations do not have to reinvent the wheel each time they engage in an activity. They also free up more time for processes to be measured and improved. But standardization is not value-free: it is not purely instrumental and neutral in the exercise of power. The concept of command and control is about the transmission of intent, most familiar in Western societies with top-down vertical hierarchies and their bureaucracies. For all the rhetoric of the business world inviting more inclusive participation in decision-making processes, ultimate responsibility resides at the apex of any hierarchy—as the saying goes, 'the buck stops here'.

Standardization also affects language and the capacity for reflection. Language or coded communication reaches most people to maximum effect when it is common to all users and exists in an agreed and recognizable form. Hence the English language has become a lingua franca of world cultural exchange, trade, and politics. This has advantaged Britain and other English-speaking countries. Indeed, on a national level, according to the sociologist Benedict Anderson, a single hegemonic language expressed in a country's vernacular and circulated in its own literature among a literate community would become the prerequisite for establishing the 'imagined community' of the 19th-century nation state.[8] By extension, exporting the operating system of Microsoft to computer desktops and laptops in most factories, offices, schools, and homes throughout the world has given that American firm and the United States a power denied to potential competitors. This echoes the removal of the gold standard in the early 1970s, which gave the United States a new lingua franca, a similar tool of influence to when the US dollar became the world's currency of default. With the trade in the dollar came also Washington's power to regulate the conditions of using that dollar.

Communication but also the vehicle through which it is distributed have been the object of struggle and appropriation for millennia. Political elites and governments have sought to preserve their competitive advantage by restricting access to a set of codes owned by privileged groups. The distribution of printed texts into a commercial marketplace was made possible by a small emerging merchant class. It followed the introduction of the printing press into Europe in the 15th century—an innovation which challenged the status quo dominated by an ecclesiastical class. Monastic scribes employed a de facto monopoly over specialist know-how in producing manuscripts in the elite language of Latin. When the Protestant Reformation challenged Roman Catholic hegemony, it chose mass print manufacture as its weapon and vernacular language as its conduit. To speak to all people in their everyday language and no longer exclusively in the hidden, if not unattainable, language of the educated was to invite a sympathetic hearing from new audiences. In response, the Church in Rome chose to adapt slowly. It continued to employ its existing workforce, its army of trained scribes, to produce handwritten manuscripts. But it embraced the new printing press too as a means for standardizing the output from the Church while mechanizing and multiplying the printed word for a more general circulation.

The state has always been an information gatekeeper, most apparent when it adopts the role of censor. Its purpose is if not quite to standardize then to reduce heterogeneity, to constrain the field of potential dissent, and to inject friction into the flow of protest. Language and censorship combined to create their own battlefield in the English Civil War of the 1640s. Babel, the biblical image of chaos and disorder, was a popular metaphor of the time. It occurs frequently in the pamphlet wars that exploded during the struggle between Protestants and the Puritan forces of Cromwell, and supporters of the Catholic monarchy of the Stuart family. It came to equate the profusion of voices and dissent with Babel or the polyglossia we still refer to as 'babble'. Thomas Hobbes, the political philosopher, writing in *Leviathan*, makes a scientific and moral plea for one single language that avoids confusion. And that language should be overseen by the sovereign:

> The Invention of Printing, though ingenious, compared with the invention of Letters, is no great matter. ... But all this language gotten, and augmented by Adam and his posterity, was again lost at the tower of Babel, when by the hand of God, every man was stricken for his rebellion, with an oblivion of his former language.[9]

As one scholar puts it, by extension, 'Babel represented competition among different languages for political legitimacy'.[10] In 1647, the royalist William Prynne published *New-Babels Confusion*. He compared parliament's deliberations over a petition titled *An Agreement of the People*, and its call that supreme power be vested in the people, to the biblical account of chaos. As James Holstun suggests:

> The Royalist attacks on the press may be seen as criticisms of the entry of new voices into the political arena, and the likening of the press's activity to Babel was a way of opposing the notion that the people were an audience fit to participate in public debate at all. The example of Babel was cited to enlist the support for a conservative antidote to the anarchy of both language and government.[11]

Each state censor and act of censorship acts as a hydraulic valve on the conduit of information passing into the public space. As the English Civil War and the French Revolution drew closer, these conduits would be overwhelmed with the sheer volume of print. An explosion of printed material in pre-revolutionary France and in republican writings during the French Revolution saw pamphleteering as an inextricable part of the spread of revolution. Government controls were subsequently tightened, mirroring similar policies under the monarchy before 1789 and causing publishing output to drop off at the height of the revolutionary Great Terror.

The more technologies—understood as carriers of information—came on stream, the more difficult it became to control thought and dissent. The more networked transport infrastructure grew, the more sources, carriers, and ideas that challenged the state connected to one other, creating a web of vectors and organic movement. Consequently, the more difficult it became to control rebellious thinking, and, so, the more necessary to introduce networked technologies of surveillance and self-censorship.[12]

## Regulation and diffusion

Mechanical reproduction introduces the idea of a multiplier effect. To produce copies of a prototype—of a city map, for example—manpower or number of machines or processes must increase. That may still cost more time, depending on how labour, machines, and processes are combined. Later, broadcast technologies such as radio, cinema, and television required more consumers to have more receiving devices in order to produce copies and proliferate the message beyond a fixed space. But with the advent of microprocessor-driven digital technologies, multiplication becomes exponential in scale-free networks. Exponential reproduction, which more recent technologies like mobile phones and laptops and the World Wide Web allow, functions via a different rationale. Here the underlying language expressed as code is standardized into zeros and ones, even if the national spoken language is overlaid, so to speak. Code language can capture picture, sounds, and words into this binary of zeros and ones. And states own the infrastructure itself—such as the internet that sits under the World Wide Web. Other platforms, like satellites and broadcast networks, may be owned by firms and their shareholders but are regulated to varying degrees by states.

When messages circulate through networks, so-called network effects are produced. That means two people talking to each other produce 2 lines of communication; three people produce 6 lines; four people produce 12 lines; five produce 18 lines; and so on. This network effect was recognized in a paper written in 1917 by N. Lytkins of the Bell Telephone Company in the United States. For the company, this multiplier effect in communications had the commercial potential to attract ever more subscribers to their phone network.

The case with Facebook is similar: it hopes to attract new sign-ups or users every day. Global commercial success has been based on signing up as many subscribers or followers as possible in order to grow the size and reach of the company. Facebook, whose declared mission is 'to give people the power to share and make the world more open and connected', claims 2.9 billion people used their service in a single month in the second quarter of 2021, and since 2018, over 1 billion use Instagram monthly.[13] Yet continued success depends not just on adequate growth, but a certain level of growth. Fast growth and the firm survives. Slow growth and it eventually loses momentum and gradually dies. The explosion in messaging potential every second of every day, when the original message can be copied and transmitted in digits around the world in split seconds by billions of mobile phone and laptop users, is dramatic. States puzzle over this growth. And they don't like it. But there is little or nothing they can do about it other than to apply the traditional, albeit updated, approaches to censorship, control, and threat of sanctions over the flows of information or over its producers and users.

When standardization and exponentiality are taken together, how does this affect Lefebvre's understanding of the state as a construct of mapping in space?[14] Perhaps it is more relevant to ask: is the state better understood as a mapping in time, not space—indeed, as an exercise in vertical mapping in time? Elias Canetti describes time as the greatest asset of the state.[15] Since it controls our lives by first segmenting, then standardizing time in various ways: the school day; the office day; the factory day; the holiday; the days of the week and months of the year; the working life; and, ethically and legally, when we can live and when we can die. The relationship between time and space—that is to say, between speed and distance—impact how ideas may be reproduced and flow between people, and how they are constrained, too.

Microprocessor-driven technologies are central to all dimensions of the process known as globalization. Besides bringing about a political assault on state regulation, or the opening up of protected economies and markets in the developing world, or accelerated and dynamic forms of moving money around the world's financial markets, and distorting how global cultural influences and local traditions interact, the advance of digital technologies has resulted in what Anthony Giddens terms 'instantaneous interconnectivity' and what Paul Virilio describes as the 'tyranny of immediacy, ubiquity, instantaneity'.[16] But what underpins this process is a productive interaction between networking and vertical regulation that long pre-existed these specific technological forms.

Back in the 1970s the management theorist Peter Drucker observed that computers and microprocessors were establishing themselves at the heart of our societies to such a degree that they were changing the way we think and behave. Drucker says this constituted a 'drastic shift to industries based not only on new and different technologies, but on *different science, different logic, and different perception*. They are also different in their workforce for they demand knowledge workers rather than manual workers.'[17] At the heart of this transformation was information. Societies were moving from a manufacturing economy to a knowledge economy. And its most prized asset was information. It had become the 'central capital, the cost centre and the crucial resource of the economy'. The distribution of power and social organization in capitalist societies and advanced economies has followed this shift in recent decades from manufacturing goods to creating knowledge. Information had become the end in itself.

This argument would be refined by the sociologist Manuel Castells. He argues that in the 1980s capitalism restructured itself, creating a new techno-economic system that he calls 'informational capitalism'. Here, access to information would determine whether individuals were inside or outside the loop of power, and whether subsequently they could access political and economic resources.[18] The net effect, according to Ankie Hoogvelt, is a rearrangement in

> the architecture of world order. Economic, social and power relations have been recast to resemble not a pyramid but a three-tier structure of concentric circles. All three circles cut across national and regional boundaries. In the core circle we find the elites of all continents. ... They are encircled by a fluid, larger social layer who labour in insecure forms of employment, thrown into cut-throat competition in the global market. ... The third, and largest, concentric circle comprises those who are already effectively excluded from the global system.[19]

This structure would not just capture the recalibration of vertical power relations between knowledge elites and subaltern classes. Whether included or excluded, it played out on the affective, imaginative domain of the individual's mind. Maps that could make sense of the world were no longer available to all. Individuals would see themselves differently in their own state and vis-à-vis the rest of the world, questioning their identity and role in society, according to maps that fitted their location. This was no uniform outcome. As the anthropologist Arjun Appadurai observes, we are conditioned not so much by face-to-face contact in real life, but rather by how we live in various imagined spaces. He labels these 'scapes'. And they break down, he says, into ethnoscapes, mediascapes, technoscapes, finanscapes, and ideoscapes. The way individuals imagine the world varies dramatically from one person to the next within any one of these five scapes, then differently as the individual moves between them.[20] Appadurai explains that he sees them as:

> deeply perspectival constructs, inflected very much by the historical, linguistic, and political situatedness of different sorts of actors: nation-states, multinationals, diasporic communities, as well as sub-national groupings and movements (whether religious, political or economic), and even intimate face-to-face groups, such as villages, neighbourhoods and families. ... These landscapes thus, are the building blocks of what, extending Benedict Anderson, we may call 'imagined worlds', that is the multiple worlds which are constituted by the historically situated imaginations of persons and groups spread around the globe.[21]

Where ideas and images are disseminated via digital technologies, the technologies determine the means by which information becomes knowledge, allowing people to make sense of the world. Ideas and images are further structured by our maps, which shape the way individuals think, not through a harmonizing diffusion but, paradoxically, through disjuncture, through flows of images that simultaneously support and challenge state hegemony. States set 'the terms on which new regimes and technologies can be received', and always seek to align them to their own vision of social order.[22] It means that states themselves are complicit in their exposure to ways of seeing that contradict their vertical ideal.

Anthony Giddens famously describes states as 'containers of power'. He points to two competing strategies of state formation. *Territorial rulers* continually expand the size of their container to increase their power. *Capitalist rulers*, however, stuff the existing container full with wealth until the needs of capital demand that the container be expanded.[23] German sociologist Ulrich Beck adds that the container has now sprung a leak, transcended by transnational connectivity.[24] Is that true? The argument usually runs like this: the climate of neoliberal reforms since the 1980s has overwhelmed states, forcing them to deregulate markets and allowing free markets to set the agenda in highly volatile, less than predictable contagions of economic panic. This has led to a tendency to confuse the semantics of liberalization—meaning freer markets through deregulation—suggesting fewer government rules. Steven Vogel observes that 'in most cases of "deregulation", governments have combined liberalization with *reregulation*, the reformulation of old rules and the creation of new ones. Hence we have wound up with freer markets and *more* rules. In fact, there is often a logical link: liberalisation requires reregulation.'[25] The relationship between states and markets is not, as is commonly assumed, a zero-sum game; it is a game of coalition.

What we're actually looking at is simply another manifestation of the state form, this time in an explicitly entrepreneurial guise.[26] The salient feature of this 'market state' is as enabler not provider: 'Market states say: Give us power and we will give you new opportunities. In contrast to the nation state, the market state does not see itself as more than a minimal provider or redistributor of goods and services.'[27] Here we see how artificial it is to counterpose networks to hierarchies. For the two have always been symbiotic. The networked entrepreneurial or market state simply reflects the way the state has continually evolved and adjusted to meet the networking economic and technological pressures of every age.

## Whose network?

In an article in *Time* magazine in 1995, Stewart Brand, creator of the Whole Earth Catalog, would famously declare, 'we owe it all to the hippies', going on to argue that the real legacy of the sixties generation was the computer revolution:

> Newcomers to the Internet are often startled to discover themselves not so much in some soulless colony of technocrats as in a kind of cultural Brigadoon—a flowering remnant of the '60s, when hippie

communalism and libertarian politics formed the roots of the modern cyber revolution. At the time, it all seemed dangerously anarchic (and still does to many), but the counterculture's scorn for centralized authority provided the philosophical foundations of not only the leaderless Internet but also the entire personal-computer revolution.[28]

From the counterculture would emerge the modern internet and World Wide Web. Not forgetting also some of the richest corporations the capitalist world had ever seen. Names like Microsoft, Google, and Apple enjoy annual turnovers and market valuations that dwarf the gross national product of many of the world's sovereign states. And individual entrepreneurs—digital innovators of the second and third generations—like Bill Gates, Steve Jobs, and Mark Zuckerberg would become modern-day heroes, the epitome of those who shook off convention, backed their own hunches, and did it their way. Theirs was a brand of pure capitalism that would revolutionize the free market. If they could achieve astronomical success from modest beginnings, then why couldn't the bloated and lethargic state take a leaf out of their books?

The truth is somewhat different. For these entrepreneurs did not hesitate to draw on the state's chequebook to kick-start their enterprises and bankroll many of the innovations from which they would piece together their popular consumer products. As Fred Turner reminds us, when the Apple Macintosh computer was launched in 1984, it was 'explicitly marketed as devices one could use to tear down bureaucracies and achieve individual intellectual freedom'.[29] This was somewhat disingenuously or even dishonestly consistent with the ethos of the New Communalists. Nevertheless it was the meeting point where counterculture interfaced with high state technology.

Lest we forget, the role of the American military in the internet's origins is central, rooted in a modest US Department of Defense network project called ARPANET (the name is derived from the Advanced Research Projects Agency), which sought to connect several research locations across the United States into one network that could connect millions of computers and users. From ARPANET would emerge the internet by the end of 1990, and the open internet would soon carry the first web page. Tim Berners-Lee declared the commercial World Wide Web open and free of charge to anyone. His was altruism of the first magnitude given a competitive world of big business and super-wealthy entrepreneurs. Its potential chimed with technology pioneers after the Second World War who aspired to computers being an extension of man—a human computer—and the symbiotic blend of cyber and communications into a new field of cybernetics. The idea that everything was part of a connected system had also registered with Stewart Brand in the 1960s. On the University of California campus at Berkeley, selling, for 25 cents a time, badges with the message 'why haven't we seen a photograph of the whole earth yet?', Brand tried to convince students that 'a photograph would do it—a color photograph from space of the earth. There it would be for all to see, the earth complete, tiny, adrift and no one would ever perceive things the same way.' On each small badge was big picture thinking.[30] Connected, we're all in this together.

The Web Foundation website sets out the web's key precepts, which remain true to its pioneer thinkers:[31] 'decentralization'—no central authority; 'non-discrimination', or net neutrality—regardless of what you pay for your connection, everyone's communication is equal; 'bottom-up design'—code is written by the greatest number openly and shared; 'universality'—computers speak the same language cutting across hardware and cultural and political differences; and 'consensus'—universal standards accrued from sharing in the common creative process. This principled vision is not universally representative of today's information industries. Those who ride on the back of the free web frequently make fortunes from its existence while manufacturing the information and computer technologies which serve it.

And much of that wealth creation is made possible by the state through its support and investment in these selfsame new technologies. Here was how success already sounded in late 2015 when *The Economist* magazine described the 'creed of speed':

> A customer downloads an app from Apple every millisecond. The firm sells 1,000 iPhones or Macs every couple of minutes. It whips through its inventories in four days and launches a new product every four weeks. Manic trading by computers and speculators means the average Apple share changes hands every five months.[32]

Today Apple is the world's richest company. Where does that success originate? Apple's Mac, iPod, iPhone, and iPad are world leaders in brand and design appeal. But beneath the aesthetics of their user-friendly packages, the internal mechanics are far from home-grown creations or even self-financed; at least they weren't in their infancy. As Mariana Mazuccato argues: 'Apple's new generation of iPods, iPhones and iPads have been built under the assumption that new consumer needs and preferences can be invented by hybridizing existing technologies developed after decades of government support.'[33] Perhaps the greatest insight that Apple brought to the marketplace was to reveal to users that telephones, particularly the recent innovation of the mobile phone, did not have to be simply for speech communication. Rather, they could 'integrate cellular communication, mobile computing and digital entertainment technologies within a single device'.[34] iPhones could now connect apps and the Global Positioning System (GPS), allowing users to access information on entertainment venues or workplace destinations while staying on the move and handling a portable device. However, Apple gained not just user advantage but hidden investment. GPS was a US Department of Defense technology invented for pinpoint accurate mapping and continues to be developed by the US Air Force; it still costs Washington some $705 million each year.

Similarly, Siri, a speech-based virtual personal assistant, is a recent addition to the Apple repertoire. But it too is the product of a collaboration between Stanford Research Institute International (hence Siri) and the US government's DARPA (Defense Advanced Research Projects Agency), intended for military personnel. Stanford Research would recognize its commercial potential for mobile telephony and set up a company to exploit the technology, Siri, Inc, which was bought out by Apple in 2010.[35] The point here is to demonstrate that there is no separation between the state and the market, even if market corporations claim the credit for innovation and risk investment. Governments constantly support ideas and product creation on which the market is reluctant to take risks and for which private investors on the whole are too small to provide funding. The sole axiom of capitalism is endless flexibility: 'capitalism has never been a static system that follows a fixed set of rules, characterized by a permanent division of responsibilities between private enterprise and governments. ... Instead, capitalism is an adaptive social system that mutates and evolves in response to a changing environment.'[36]

There is a temptation to default to reading the relationship between information and the state as one defined by the state's directive attempts to map and control the domain of digital technologies and cyberspace. Intrusion also comes from the opposite direction. Witness the scientific mapping of the human genome, where the partnership between state and market functions differently. Between 1975 and around 2001, two different projects emerged aiming to sequence the human genome, the biological blueprint of each human life. On the one hand, the Human Genome Project was an international cooperative team underpinned by private philanthropy and government funding. Theirs, put simply, was a Baconian view of science: knowledge for the sake of knowledge, or at least for the free benefit of mankind. On the other hand, there was Celera Genomics Corporation, a commercial research organization. Exclusive rights to access its future patents and data deriving from mapping human life would be the trade-off for guaranteeing substantial investment from big pharmaceutical corporations and the stock market. The firm would be bankrolled throughout its research years. And in return the market expected a healthy return on its extremely risky and costly investment.[37]

Racing to the finishing line, the excitement of such brilliant research was accompanied by an ethical debate: could or should the map of life be owned by the private sector? Surely the genomic map was common property, a commons—a mirror of nature—a discovery, not an invention? To subject it to enclosure and to commoditize its data, no less to charge future scientists money to access or use it, was surely unethical. Such concerns resonate with debates about the internet as a virtual space, albeit made up of hardwired infrastructure owned and regulated by states and private companies. Public and the private sectors contest this space each day, attempting to enclose it in a spirit reminiscent of the enclosures that marked the transition from feudalism to capitalism between the 1400s and 1800s. Similarly, market firms now set up gated communities in virtual space and charge pay-per-view subscriptions to use them.

The spirit of the commons imagined by utopian cyber pioneers is threatened by the International Telecommunications Union (ITU), a United Nations agency. In 2012 in Dubai, member states were divided on extending the remit of the ITU to include regulating the internet. To date, the way internet governance has been understood is through a 'multi-stakeholder' process. That means that an alliance of states, such as China, India, Iran, Russia, and Saudi Arabia, could seek to wrest control from what they view as the grasp of the United States and other Western countries. Their desire was to gain greater access to cyberspace through an intergovernmental agency. India tabled a proposal that internet access should be gained via dial-ups with national prefixes, similar to familiar and long-standing international telephone dialling. This would have the effect of corralling internet traffic within sovereign national borders. So, accessing sites outside the country would require a dedicated and deliberate act for each time it was used.

As much as this cluster of states has been resisted by the United States and its more libertarian allies, from a different perspective, Germany sees its own notion of the internet as 'a public good and a public space'. This vision was deeply threatened by the revelations of whistle-blower Edward Snowden: 'The[se] ... confirmed what everyone already knew ... that, contra conventional wisdom around the seemingly chaotic or unorganizable nature of digital systems, the internet is in fact the mostly highly controlled mass media hitherto known'.[38] Shocking revelations opened up a dark world where Washington's security agencies had been caught spying on the German chancellor Angela Merkel and her government officials using mobile phone and internet intercepts. Germany officially favours the discourse of a spontaneous, bottom-up creativity rather than the top-down regulation that extending powers to the ITU would inevitably bring. Even these assumptions should be queried, says Alexander Galloway:

It is common for contemporary critics to describe the internet as an unpredictable mass of data ... lacking central organization. This position states that since new communication technologies are based on the

elimination of centralized command and hierarchical control, it follows
that the world is witnessing a general disappearance of control as such.
This could not be further from the truth.[39]

The internet is a decentralized space with little bureaucratic command—
that is true. But it is not a space free from control. Internet protocols
'refer specifically to standards governing the implementation of specific
technologies', creating standards that are adopted and implemented globally.
And so they act as 'conventional rules that govern a set of possible behavior
patterns within a heterogeneous system'.[40] Decentralized regulation makes
possible the physical transference of data packages and renders it possible
for them to be received. This system works only because of the continuous
tension between state mapping hierarchies (vertical architecture of
DNS—Domain Name System) and distributed network maps (horizontal
architecture of TCP/IP—Transmission Control Protocol/Internet Protocol).
These are the pragmatic means by which the internet allows for control
alongside radical decentralization, including the potential removal of entire
geographical zones from the net at the behest of states. Here the unmapping
of both state and network are in action.

Popular enthusiasm for hackers, from libertarian technological billionaire
elites to leftist ideologues,[41] is rooted in the idea that they are 'Freedom
Fighters, living by the dictum that data wants to be free', personifying faith
that decentralization is an unalloyed good.[42] Their transformation in the
public mind since the 1970s into election fiddlers, terrorists, perpetrators of
state-sponsored bank heists, criminals, childish spammers, viral marketers,
conspiracy theorists, trolls, and misogynistic ideologues captures only
one aspect of the problem. The ethos of hacking is simply to exploit the
possibilities that subsist within the vertical and horizontal protocols which
together organize the internet.[43]

John Perry Barlow's 'Declaration of the Independence of Cyberspace'[44]
demanded that the internet would be inherently rooted in freedom, both
functionally and causally. These are the same values professed by billionaire
figures in the tech industry, such as Elon Musk, Peter Theil, and Eric
Schmidt. Their commitment to freedom from government regulation
also highlights monopolistic control over market-capturing platforms and
technologies.[45] Big data-gathering platforms, like Facebook, Google, and
Palantir, contradict the vertical state map.[46] They show that the state map
cannot be adequate, because the state now urgently needs their services.
Consequently, they have become the clearest advocates of a networked
system of governance, supported by a global technocratic elite that makes
the internet work by designing its protocols.

Their commitment to a networked, entangled non-linearity, however,
masks the important ways in which 'control has existed from the beginning',[47]

which looks nothing like the state map. 'Control in distributed networks is not monolithic. It proceeds in multiple, parallel, contradictory, and often unpredictable ways.'[48] Failure to grasp that horizontal distribution is a map which carries with it various architectures for control has given birth to a misplaced utopian faith in networks.

We live in an era where certainties of the international system of sovereign states are no longer apparent. The result is a 'blurring of all citadel structures, from the state, to the aura and authority of works of art, to the solemn autonomy of the ego, within the expanding and directed environment of information'.[49] Transnational flows and networks continuously circumvent and interact with state hierarchies within this infrastructure. They remain deeply complicit in how states continue to adapt in spaces where information, networks, hierarchies, and markets vie for control.

**Figure 8.1:** Moscow Metro map 2030

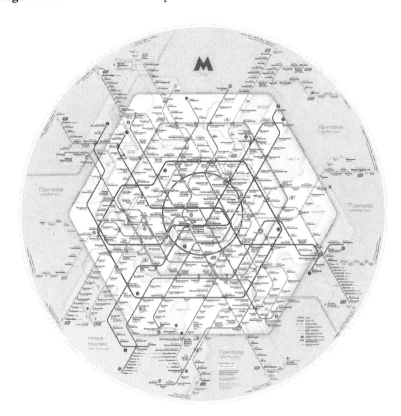

Source: Constantine Konovalov and Natalia Moskaleva (2021)

8

# Romance of Networks

Andrew Culp, remarking on popular celebrations of maps of network connectivity, suggests that 'the first step is to acknowledge that the unbridled optimism for connection has failed. Temporary autonomous zones have become special economic zones. The material consequences of connectivity are clear: the terror of exposure, the diffusion of power, and the oversaturation of information.'[1] Rather than embrace a romance of networks, Culp suggests breaking their circuits, rejecting transparency, and questioning the 'techno-affirmationist dream' of networks as inherently liberating.[2]

The problem becomes unpicking our faith in our cherished maps, vertical and horizontal. As Janet Abrams and Peter Hall suggest:

> mapping has emerged in the information age as a means to make the complex accessible, the hidden visible, the unmappable mappable. As we struggle to steer through the torrent of data unleashed by the internet, and to situate ourselves in a world in which commerce and community have been redefined in terms of networks, mapping has become a way of making sense of things.[3]

Yet, they continue, the 'network when viewed from above, faces the same charge of misrepresentation that Harley and a generation of critical cartographers levelled at the bird's eye view'.[4] Network maps omit to recall that maps are never a mirror of the territory they represent. Faith in the utopia of networks is far from new:[5]

> from their earliest social applications, networks based on technical support invariably appeared to be the basis of new types of exchange between people, of a new democracy. Their ramifications appeared to irrigate a vast community, overcoming isolation, parochialism and vagaries of climate. Such a belief is already apparent in 1794 with installation in revolutionary France of the first optical and signal

telegraph line, invented by the Chappe brothers. Some revolutionaries dreamed of putting the future lines 'at the service of the great democratic republics'. Capable of 'communicating their information and their intentions over great distances, so to speak, instantaneously', the citizens could revive the agora, but were no longer limited as in Athens to the public square. Disillusion was quick to set in. In reality the optical telegraph was put to use in the service of those in power. The technique quickly proved its strategic utility by connecting Paris to its fortresses and revolutionary armies.[6]

Nonetheless it remains a common belief that the network map tends politically towards: free and open interaction; decentralized or consensus democratic decision-making; self-organizing from the bottom up, not the top down; and consequently liberation.

Throughout this book, hierarchies and networks form intricate relationships in different hybrid formations. This is noticeable in the People's Global Action network, which evolved into the 'alter-globalization movement', which in turn became the World Social Forum, hoping to 'create within the organization the structures, practices, and relationships you strive to create in the world'.[7] It was a movement for which decentralization and horizontal organization explicitly shaped a map for politics. Adopting a loose structure for swarming through decentralized global networks, their internal governance was framed by direct participatory democracy and an anarchistic ethos.[8] Yet even here hierarchies proliferated.

Anarchist writer David Graeber argues that the tactics of antiglobalization were explicitly 'less about seizing state power than about exposing, delegitimizing and dismantling mechanisms of rule while winning ever-larger spaces of autonomy from it'.[9] This might embody types of direct democracy that are anti-authoritarian and consensual in spirit. But, more important, they could be read in a visual form.[10] This reached its apogee in the Occupy movement. Drawing on the experience of Indymedia and the anti-globalization and global social justice movements, Occupy pushed to create new spaces. It was a politics to mirror-image its map: horizontal, networked, local. When *Adbusters* magazine urged protesters to occupy Wall Street on 13 July 2011, a series of events dominoed with the shared aim of occupying a square of public space, believing the act prefigured a new world of decentralized networking, non-hierarchical organization and 'DIY politics'.[11] Central to their belief was the idea that they were imitating participatory general assemblies that evoked the Greek agora. Visibility of the politics of space, impossible to grasp using the map of state, drove how the movement understood itself and claimed to do things differently.

Claims that these movements were free from vertical structures and opposed to the map of the sovereign state were overstated. As Paolo

Gerbaudo, with agreement from many others, observes, 'the use of the internet and social media within contemporary social movements [often] brings about new forms of soft and distributed leadership'.[12] Hierarchy was never absent from these networks; it was simply hidden from view, as 'leadership groups, and digital vanguards are largely responsible for setting up, by giving movements collective names, by coining a series of hashtags, of icons, of internet memes, and in so doing constructing a basic operational identity'.[13] Hierarchies permeate all effective or ineffective protest networks. When combined with a 'deterministic understanding and use of technology', faith in the visibility of an anti-state map made decision-making difficult.[14] Moreover, it precluded long-time planning and building social movements. Maps created online to reflect online ideals were simply transposed onto perceptions of the real space of protest.

Leaderlessness need not be a problem for an insurgent. There is more than one way to organize against the state. But falling for the network map is a trap into which horizontalist political movements often stumble. This was evidenced in Tunisia and Egypt during the Arab Spring after 2010, where fundamentalist religious associations, trade unions, and football associations survived as hierarchies within the wider uprising. Yet they were ignored in news reports that preferred to present protests as the universal spirit of a networked global revolution. Part of the problem is simply the complexity of mapping the ways the vertical and horizontal interact in any protest movement.[15]

The romance of networks hides distinct forms of control that pervade every network. Digital networks are simply 'structures for a negotiated dominance of certain flows over other flows', or in other words, spaces where control operates through gatekeeping as well as vertical command.[16] Management operates differently through networks. Which creates spaces to some degree hostile to overarching hierarchy and centralization. Yet control is not absent.

The network map is an inadequate tool for making sense of filters that determine the internet's often reactionary political content. Believing that performing the map can stand in for politics, networks breed political engagement that inclines towards theatricality. Providing a space for voicing grievance, it fails to direct the expression of that grievance.[17] Texts that imagine horizontal swarming through a carnival of protest will deliver a happier globalism[18] rarely consider the possibility that the swarm may not necessarily reflect how pluralist democratic politics are conducted.[19] Indeed, it has appeared particularly problematic in light of the rise of populist, racist, and misogynist 'autonomous zones' online.[20] Not to mention spectacular protests like the invasion of America's White House in 2020, which captured the networked form of horizontal distribution.

Swarming creates a rich environment to proliferate paranoia and conspiracies. Alongside resilience, spontaneity, and horizontalism, it provides the dominant trope of far right 'leaderless resistance'.[21] Beam, the chief far right strategist of decentralization, was among the first to reject hierarchical organization:

> the pyramid, is ... not only useless, but extremely dangerous for the participants when it is utilized in a resistance movement against state tyranny. Especially is this so in technologically advanced societies where electronic surveillance can often penetrate the structure revealing its chain of command. Experience has revealed over and over again that anti-state, political organizations utilizing this method of command and control are easy prey for government infiltration, entrapment, and destruction of the personnel involved. This has been seen repeatedly in the United States where pro-government infiltrators or agent provocateurs weasel their way into patriotic groups and destroy them from within. ... Like the fog which forms when conditions are right and disappears when they are not, so must the resistance to tyranny be.[22]

Contest between the maps of state and network belongs to both left and right. Slippage occurs between the two, rooted in the urge to 'liberate the flows'.[23] Political effects attached to network maps are open to every taste. All are sets of 'technical procedures' to be integrated and managed,[24] regulating informational flows towards a variety of political functions.[25]

The internet sits at the intersection between hierarchy and swarm. Horizontalist actors who emerge, intervene in, and resist state regulation are diverse. Some would decolonize society, while others are racist; some are feminists, while others hate women. 'There is no need for fear or hope', as Deleuze once said. The horizontal network has always been present, forever at work with, across, between, and against vertical hierarchies. Yet the pervasiveness of conspiratorial 'pastiche and repetition' in online communities is an effect of network which reinforces Walter Benjamin's argument about the relationship between politics and aesthetic paradigms. Here, in Marshall McLuhan's words, 'the medium is the message'. Networked conspiracies from the Illuminati to the Great Replacement to QAnon reflect ever faster technological reproducibility of maps. Downloading allows conspiratorial maps to eclipse the very world they claim to represent.[26] Frederick Jameson hopes that 'an aesthetics of cognitive mapping' could resolve our incapacity to grasp the networks in which we are now entangled.[27] Precisely because of our commitment to network mapping, hipster reactionary aesthetics of the new right and swarming conspiracy theories proliferate. After all, as he goes on to suggest, conspiracy is the definitive form of network mapping, seeking to capture the whole[28] yet swarm-like, resilient to critique, and open to endless variation.[29]

What is labelled the alt-right merges into a leaderless, distributed network, including a range of movements and figures from neo-Nazis, white supremacists, anti-feminists, paleochristian conservatives, to neo-reactionaries.[30] This assemblage demonstrates why 'networked, leaderless Internet-centric politics now seems a little less worthy of uncritical celebration'.[31] Transgression of the state form by horizontally networking subcultures online is the central concern for most core works of the 'self-evidently different—and only precariously compatible' neo-reactionary alt-right online.[32] Which brings to an end the age of innocence for the network map, all-channel and horizontally distributed.[33]

## Secrecy and faith

Every city is a city of flows, binding together multiple networks, as beautifully illustrated in the futurist imagining of Moscow which began this chapter. Urban social movements have emerged to protest racism, state restrictions on assembly, and global environmental calamity. They are connected with patterns of dependency and vulnerability to the state, and rooted in the legacies of history. Such movements embrace a politics of communicative action, seeking to influence and redirect state action. The need for visibility and engagement with the state are expressed in the pursuit of maximum publicity through protests and non-violent action.

This politics of visibility contrasts sharply with a group of French anarchists arrested on 11 November 2008 for involvement in a series of secretive sabotage actions against high-speed train lines; they were later acquitted. A key plank of the prosecutors' case was their alleged authorship of a book entitled *The Coming Insurrection*, which had been published anonymously under the pen name of The Invisible Committee.[34] The text was considered uniquely threatening to the state.

The Invisible Committee wrote from an understanding of the state as intrinsically open to disturbance. Today's urban society is thought of as an 'architecture of flows' rendering it 'one of the most vulnerable human arrangements that has ever existed. Supple, Subtle, but vulnerable. ... The world would not be moving so fast if it didn't have to constantly outrun its own collapse.'[35] The networked 'science of control' already holds the potential for strategic counteractions. The text suggests an alternative strategy for the state challenger, namely to 'jam everything'. Even the most resilient state networks are not 'invulnerable to all destruction'. Recognizing that 'every network has its weak points, the nodes that must be undone in order to interrupt circulation, to unwind the web', The Invisible Committee calls for a campaign of sabotage to attack the very networks modern society believes underpin its resilience:

the technical infrastructure of the metropolis is vulnerable. Its flows amount to more than the transportation of people and commodities

... sabotaging the social machine with any real effect involves re-appropriating and reinventing the ways of interrupting the network. How can a TGV line or an electrical network be rendered useless? How does one find the weak points in computer networks, or scramble radio-waves and fill screens with white noise?[36]

States' pursuit of a strategy of resilience by decentralizing—through just-in-time production, for example—is what opens them to strategic confrontation. A strategy of continuous interruption replaces that of major interruption.

The Invisible Committee's appeal was to 'block the economy', avoiding at all costs being seen and any direct confrontation with the state. Swarming is placed centre stage in an attempt to create 'a moving multiplicity that can strike a number of places at once and that tries to always keep the initiative'. To occupy space is to fail to attack an already swarming state. The secret to success is to interrupt the system, its *'perpetuum mobile'*, so that alternative networks can be constructed.[37] This parasitic response is seen as a way of radicalizing self-organization that occurs in any moment of crisis, as was seen in New Orleans after Hurricane Katrina or in local communities worldwide distributing food to those self-isolating or particularly vulnerable to pandemic coronavirus. Rather than territorial occupation, counter-state structures were built in alternative sources of aid and education that occupy the same territory as the state but are always out of sight of states.

The authors of *The Coming Insurrection* thought they should disrupt the normal flow of the city, then use 'moments of instability ... to consolidate or strengthen' and replace one network with another. Any 'interruption of the flows' would allow them to replace networks to prevent the old from being rebuilt. This explains, they say, why Islamist movements like Hamas are successful: they mobilize crisis for self-organization, providing assistance, education, and social support, beyond the state networks' ability to reform. Territory should not be occupied physically. Resistance builds only from a strategy of mobile resilience, 'increasing the density of the communes of circulation, and of solidarities to the point that the territory becomes unreadable, opaque to all authority'.[38]

Visibility for their cause is not the aim. It seeks 'an invulnerable position of attack .... No leader, no demands, no organization, but words, gestures, complicities. To be socially nothing is ... the condition for maximum freedom of action.' This is because 'Power is no longer concentrated in one point in the world; it is the world itself, its flows and its avenues.' Flows must be the object and method of attack. The project to confront state resilience with counter-resilience reaches a strategic apogee: a confrontation between flows.[39] The city becomes a space for setting up a new horizontal politics. This forces the state to innovate by networking itself.

There is an echo here. Brazilian revolutionary Carlos Marighella's 'Handbook of Urban Guerrilla Warfare' advocates urban terror to spark wider rural guerrilla war.[40] Marighella thought the city was essential but never decisive in the 'complementary struggle'.[41] It was a space for diversionary techniques, to foster tension and sidetrack armed forces, preventing them from concentrating and encircling the counter-state insurgency.

Urban space is a space of vulnerability for insurgents. Marighella believed it was for the state too. In the absence of mass struggle in the city, small urban groups engage in lightning strikes, ambushes, assassinations, and sabotage; they strike at a state's unique vulnerability. Insurgent weakness is only tempered by radical decentralization: 'We have kept our organization free from complex command systems depending on internal hierarchies and a numerous and immobile bureaucracy at the top.' Innovation by small groups engaging in flexible revolutionary actions is essential to countering the inherent threat of the city. Marighella abandons the complex chain of command, instead freeing up autonomous, mobile groups who continually spring local initiatives: revolutionary decentralization allows the 'decisive moving force in the movement' to become 'the initiative of its revolutionary groups'.[42]

This spirit of initiative, violent experimentation, decentralization and networked distribution is the lasting legacy of the handbook. This manual of revolutionary swarming would spawn 'a vast and indestructible network' where every attack is followed by instant withdrawal. Harassing, demoralizing, and confusing state forces gradually erodes its capability. Consequently, it is goaded to overreact. A 'war of nerves' ensues in which the aim is to outcompete the enemy. Fragmentation and distribution enable guerrillas to out-think the states.[43]

The city moves from being a site of vulnerability for the guerrilla to one of vulnerability for the state. Confusion, fear, and uncertainty can be fostered. Here are resonances with the strategic concept behind urban terrorism— elements of networked strategy morphing into revolutionary strategic thinking. But there is also reference to earlier anarchist strategies of challenge built around distributed organization, spontaneity, and triggering a collective social uprising through violent 'Propaganda of the Deed'. Combining spectacular violence, decentralization, and horizontal networking has deep roots in the political left and right.[44]

It is tempting to suggest that strategies of visibility or secrecy simply refract the division between vertical and horizontal politics. But hyper-visible protest movements such as Extinction Rebellion, Black Lives Matter, or the conspiratorial lockdown protesters of QAnon are as committed as any group to applying horizontal maps for politics. Organized online, through decentralized systems of governance, their planning is shaped by negotiating with hierarchies.

Anarchists of the late 19th century were among the first to develop a thesis around highly visible urban Propaganda of the Deed, making use of assassinations, bombings, and sabotage to spark a wider revolutionary uprising.[45] Bakunin favours individual dedication and consciousness over broad revolutionary alliance. Only violent commitment, he argues, could establish conditions 'favourable to the awakening of popular initiative ... and shake the masses out of their sheepish state'.[46] Using destruction can awaken the 'spirit of revolt, the source of all moral and material emancipation' by translating a universal but 'blind' instinct to reject hierarchy and despotism, and awaken conscious and popular revolutionary will.[47] For Bakunin, then, public violence unleashes the revolutionary urge already immanent in the masses. Sergei Nechayev, a disciple later disowned by Bakunin, took the appeal to horizontalist spontaneity to its limit,[48] exhorting revolutionaries to break all bonds with the social order, to reject all established laws, conventions, doctrines and moralities, and to devote themselves to the task of remapping society from the ground up.

As Nicholas Kiersey and Wanda Vrasti note, Rosa Luxemburg was building on this tradition. When she 'endorses the general strike as a meaningful strategy for social change, she was moving towards the anarchist side of the debate'. But Luxemburg also 'accused anarchists of reducing the strike to a sort of starry-eyed instrumentality'. She understood it, rather, as a 'training ground for revolutionary subjectivity'. The strike aims to foster appropriate understanding in the masses by 'prefiguring' a horizontal world defined by, for example, 'self-organization, voluntary association, mutual aid'.[49] Just as the vanguardist ideal prefigured the despotic Stalinist state, the anarchist vision of revolutionary political action hoped to perform the reality of the network map; to map out through practice and in the public mind the polity it wished to bring into being. Since the 1990s, the Cyber Left has accepted this vision of politics as the foundation for realizing the network map.[50] New social media technologies are seen to encourage diverse movements, aims, and groups to be integrated into horizontal organizational swarming, to attack the state in the name of ecological justice and gender or racial pluralism.[51]

Ideas fomented in 1960s counterculture root this tradition, aiming at creating molecular spaces of self-governing. It is often forgotten that these were tied into the resurgence of new religions and cults at the time; similar to the earlier and contemporary anarchists embracing new religions— hermetic and millenarian strands of the Enlightenment—in a continuum.[52] Disastrous horizontalist experiments in the 1960s, including the Jim Jones mass suicides, underline the role of faith and mysticism in revolutionary history, symbolism, and historiography—a point Erica Lagalisse makes.[53] The 1960s saw wide-ranging experiments with wildcat strikes, university occupations, pirate radio stations, refusal to work in favour of autonomous, self-provisioning in communes—all of which sought to embody the kinds of worlds they wanted to realize, culminating in the Situationist movement which collapsed performance into politics.

The sense that politics must be performative and visible was also clear in the workers' autonomy movement, whose aim was to create molecular spaces of autonomous governing in factories, or squats. 'The Autonmen of the 1960s, 1970s, and 1980s sought to create autonomous zones through squatting, such as the Kreuzberg neighbourhood in Berlin, where housing, social centres and entire districts were squatted, transformed and defended free of the hegemonies of family, state, nuclear power and the Protestant ethic'.[54] Luxemburg's idea of the pedagogy of the general strike had been turned into a map for a 'horizontalist' future.[55] It was when the map of the 'decentralized network' moved online that it found what it thought was a perfect space of magical realization. The 'Zapatista movement integrated Mayans, Marxists, and transnational NGOs', driven by a media-based approach designed to support and give substance to this alignment.[56] The birth of Indymedia was a direct response to this call.

Set up in 1999 to report on the WTO [World Trade Organization] meetings and counter demonstrations, it was bound up with critiques of mass media as fundamentally lacking diversity. Their motto, 'don't hate the media, be the media', expressed an ethos of horizontalist prefiguration, uniting activists, programmers, independent journalists, radio states, websites and community organizers.[57]

The network map, it was hoped, could reveal the hegemonic sovereign international as a fragile monster. And new revolutionary social forces would be released to restructure and rewire national and international politics through protests on the streets of Cairo, Athens, New York, Kyiv, and London in the first decade of the 21st century. Viral collapse of authoritarian states was seen also as a challenge to the centres of global economic power: a new global 'figure of resistance' was imagined, empowered to cross cultural spaces, social movements, and geographic contexts. William Connolly confides his 'sense' that 'a variety of forces is converging creatively today towards distinctive images of activism, ecology and freedom',[58] to arise from an array of rupturing or devastating events sparked by the 2008 financial crisis.[59] Why was this cluster of events seen as a single dynamic instead of coincidental occurrences? The answer: a map could be discerned. Events appeared to share a distinctive form, one of a self-organizing crowd occupying public space. The network map with its promise to seed wider rebellion was felt to capture these events and presage a road to a global future.

Faith that the network might offer the means to transcend 'local, regional, class, racial, state and religious ... loyalties and identifications, so as to respond and self-organize to challenge local political, social, economic and "planetary" or climatic conditions', derives from the problem of mapping.[60] Faith in maps prevented consideration of how swarms arising from catastrophes give rise to second-, third-, and multiple-order effects that fold together horizontal and vertical in ever more diverse ways. Just as resurgent autocracy and populist nationalism worldwide followed the network protests of the early 2010s, similar outcomes may follow a more recent cycle of horizontal protests on the left and right—opposing the state map, but advocating racial, ecological, or identitarian liberation while embodying the network map. On this occasion, amid the shock of a global COVID-19 pandemic. Faith in maps, vertical or horizontal, is a recipe for disappointment.

## A climate for the state

Extreme weather events, more than pandemics, were until recently believed to pose the highest risk to critical networks of the state.[61] Scientists project an increase in scale of the most powerful storms of category 4 or 5.[62] They project global increases in rainfall. There is evidence too for pathway movement in powerful storms, creating uncertainty around where they will strike,[63] together with the destructive impact of weather events.[64] Alongside already projected rises in sea levels, a consensus has emerged predicting increases in the most destructive events. Climatic consequences of climate change will negatively impact the capacity of states to govern, irrespective of intergovernmental action. But they also invite solutions based on reconciling the territory with its map.

Our mechanized societies already pre-date the invention of the steam engine. It has been argued that '[a]fter 1945, there began *the Great Acceleration*, in which the geological transformation of Earth by humans increased by vivid orders of magnitude', and that acceleration in society focuses attention on complex connections between actions and consequences.[65] Acceleration requires abandoning expectations of incremental change and encourages a new awareness of the complex processes that envelop modern life.[66] It is the scale of climatic change that underpins environmental protest movements like Extinction Rebellion. Environmental movements are increasingly transnational in the 21st century, emerging as a network beyond the state. Proponents argue that people not states must self-organize to meet the climate challenge, given the evidence of states' failure to deal with the crisis.

Yet the state map has always made a powerful case to be on the side of nature. International responses to the coronavirus pandemic offer useful insights into how international society may yet become open to evolution in a direction which rearticulates, rather than opposes, the state map. Witness the practices of nationalist actors and their international allies. Notably in the United States and Brazil, nationalist leaders embraced failure in their response to the pandemic. Even here, in that failure, a space opens up for new kinds of state politics. Nature, in the form of the rights of birth, has always been central to nationalist discourse on the purpose of the state. It suggests how natural phenomena are given sense by the state map. Nationalist traditions contain a wider intellectual current of conservativism. Its responses to the French Revolution emphasized place and rootedness and accounts of identity grounded in what it meant to be born in a particular land; it placed value on the human body's intrinsic relationship to a culture contained and nurtured within state borders. The state map often makes its most powerful case for its vertical diagram at the moment when natural disasters strike, claiming only it can chart the true links between a people and the land it inhabits.

The state structure of international order provides few means by which to conceptualize the contingency of its ordering rules. Teleologically, modern states assumed extending rights to humanity as a whole—globalizing democracy, free trade, and multilateralist institutions—reflected a trend towards progress rather than accidents of history. With environmental change, a common assumption is that the only way forward is to thicken a horizontal global order; the ensuing crisis will push the train of state along the track of history towards its dissolution.

Anatol Lieven, among others, argues that to achieve the kinds of radical action that are now needed to combat unfolding climate disaster, people must be mobilized to change their lives fundamentally.[67] Vertical states provide the only tools that make this possible. Coronavirus has shown what climatic disasters can do and what the effects for everyday life may be; the appeal of this map has clearly not faded. To affect the kinds of action needed to manage viral flows cutting across state borders has required intrusive bureaucracy. The argument that only the vertical state form has the power to foster the sacrifices and collective action needed to prevent disaster, and that only the map of state can bind political control over countries with a deep identity that mobilizes populations, has as lasting and mystical appeal as the network map. After all, the state map is designed to manage and respond to crises of network flows.

That argument draws too on the failures of networked international organizations revealed by the pandemic, whether real or imagined. National bureaucracies compete and cooperate with networks in the pursuit of security from threats including climate change, migration, and crime. A network of security professionals crosses national frontiers globally. Its disciplines include what Didier Bigo calls 'an archipelago of policing'—city, criminal, customs, border control, antiterrorist—as well as intelligence agencies and counter-espionage, with diverse information technologies, surveillance, detection, and protection. A culture of data collection and interrogation unites them. Professional control over population data privileges and at the same time distances them from more accessible reaches of bureaucracy. A private and public archipelago with shared but not common experience emerges—global, networked and elite, built within states and on states—but nevertheless moves beyond the publicly accountable oversight of states.[68] President Obama's former policy planning chief in the State Department, Anne-Marie Slaughter demands we see the world not as a collection of unitary states but as disaggregated states—connected in networks of legislation, adjudication, and professional practice.[69] Her plea is for a networked world order. World government, not through centralized parliament but through obligations and oversight, through horizontally integrated bureaucratic elites, speaking to both internal and foreign constituencies. This image of a networked governance, without need for or appeal to the direct assent of populations, has become the central trope linking together online conspiracists and national populists.

As networked global institutions are perceived as unable to meet their promises in the face of climate change, people turn to alternative maps to explain failure. In the face of cataclysmic hurricanes, creeping deserts, rampant wild fires, sea level rises, scorching heatwaves, and water shortages, all of which are now seen as inevitable global consequences of previous (in)actions, faith in horizontal politics and transnational non-state activism may seem more, not less, misplaced.[70] If even the most cautious voices on the climate crisis are proven right, the situation may shortly become so acute as to render the case for the state map inescapable. Anyone refuting calls for a networked global passage beyond the world of nations may find ever larger audiences sympathetic to reinforcing borders.

Popular return to the map of state will also mask the interactions at work. International order faces a moment of unexpected confusion. In the belief that state sovereignty provided the measure of history, for both advocates and critics, a basic error was at play. Today's reactionary reformation of the international derives from a failure to consider that the state and all its actions can only be truly understood through its shifting partnerships with constitutive networks and flows.[71]

**Figure 9.1:** Map signed by Sir Mark Sykes and François Georges-Picot, enclosed in Paul Cambon's 9 May 1916 letter to Sir Edward Grey

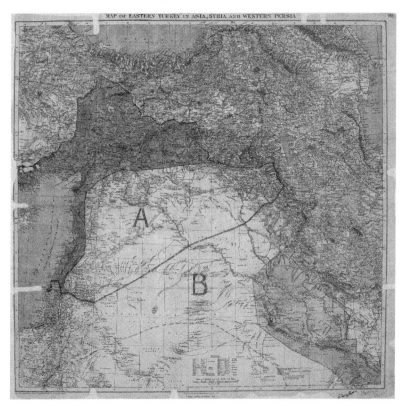

# Borders and Impermanence

President Donald Trump, before leaving office, had hoped the United States could be walled off from Mexico on its southern border to combat the flow of bodies from the south. Pressures on the borders of the European Union, a direct consequence of recent wars in Syria, Iraq, and Afghanistan, remind us of the porous and impermanent nature of all state lines. The trigger response of states on Europe's eastern front, as of the United States, defaulted to the idea that barriers be erected, made of razor wire and bricks and mortar. This idea represents a constant refrain throughout history. Long before the city of Berlin and two post-war Germanies were divided by a makeshift wall that would soon be fortified and militarized, and long before Israel built its West Bank Barrier, a separation wall to contain Palestinians and secure Israel from what it saw as the origin of terror attacks, long-forgotten empires and their rulers had attempted similar methods.

We can still walk the reminder of a line designed to hold back nomadic energy flows and protect the state of the Middle Kingdom that preceded contemporary China. The Great Wall of China has survived two thousand years of storms, aggression, and now tourism. But it is unwise to assume that what lies either side of it has been equally resilient or dyadic. Most walls come and go. Hadrian's wall dividing modern Scotland from England only survives in parts. Today, we may even be surprised to learn that such ambitious challenges to human ingenuity and engineering have ever existed. They are as forgotten as historic hegemons captured in the poet Percy Shelley's 'Ozymandias', king of kings.

Hot and cold wars were waged between the Roman and Persian empires in the 3rd and 4th centuries. This was a bipolar, geopolitical conflict between states wrapped inside another contest. That contest was between an increasingly Christianizing and expansionist Roman Empire that had relocated to its new centre in Constantinople and a revivalist Sasanian Persian Empire with its own strong Zoroastrian cosmology. By the middle of the 4th century, two dramatic events befell both combatants. First, climate change triggered widespread agricultural failure and famine. Change in temperatures afflicted all states from Eastern Europe right across Asia to China. This would have further cataclysmic and unforeseen knock-on effects. Nomadic tribes—pastoralist horsemen who made up a mosaic of tribes that originated in Mongolia and ranged across the steppes—may have shifted their areas of occupation westwards in search of new grasslands and water to stave off the effects of desertification and famine.

Regardless of the complex causes behind this wave of nomadic invaders, both empires, that spanned the terrain either side of the Bosporus—where Europe meets the Asian content—were confronted by a third force. The dominant tribe who came to be feared in Europe as the Huns conquered all their neighbours. And the first sign of unrest to be felt further afield was the arrival of mass refugees seeking new lands to settle within the territories of the Roman Empire, across the borderlands of northern contemporary Afghanistan to the western borders of the empire. Roman stability near the Danube was unsettled. According to Peter Frankopan, they would soon be followed by the arrival of Huns. In 378 CE on the open steppes of Thrace, where contemporary north-east Greece and Bulgaria meet Turkey, a massive Roman army suffered defeat at the hands of the Huns. And their commander, the Roman emperor Valens, was killed. Persia witnessed a similar fate. Its eastern lands and trade routes were overrun, towns and commercial nodes depopulated, and vital irrigation networks destroyed. Hun forces penetrated as far south as Mesopotamia and the Tigris and Euphrates in modern-day Syria and Iraq.[1]

The threat to geopolitical security in the extended region brought Persia and Roman Constantinople to a shared interest and need to cooperate. The Romans would choose to adopt a dual strategy: one, pay tribute—bribes—to the fearsome horsemen and trust they would honour the agreement not to advance further; and, two, build a wall to keep them out. The wall designed to protect the Persian Empire's interior received financial support from Constantinople plus an injection of Roman troops. Cooperation produced a 125-mile wall running between the Caspian Sea and the Black Sea, protecting Persia's northern exposure. The wall was defended by 30 forts and a canal 15 feet deep, and manned by a military force of 30,000. For the Roman Empire, however, time had run out. Displacement across the steppes north of the Black Sea led to wave upon wave of nomadic forces penetrating as far as the river Rhine, thus breaching the empire's border, before they swept south through Gaul and into contemporary Italy. In 410 CE, the Visigoth tribe sat outside the walls of Rome and, when protracted negotiations stalled, invaded and sacked the city.[2]

Compare that with Turkey's construction of a 13-foot-high wall to stretch for 50 miles along its 566-mile southern border with northern Syria. Like Israel's West Bank wall, it is fitted with searchlights, observation towers, and armed guards. Its intention is to block the advance of suicide bombers and prevent the passage of migrants from some 37 countries into Turkish territory. Ankara appears to have two militant targets in mind: Islamic State fighters and Kurdish People's Protection Unit (YPG) guerrillas with putative links to Turkey's own militant Kurdistan Workers' Party (PKK) engaged in a long-running conflict with Ankara. The YPG has also been active against the Islamic State in northern Syria. Turkey says the wall will be dismantled if and when Syria returns to peace.[3]

A rich United States, in both bureaucratic and military-industrial assets, shares a 2,000-mile border with Mexico. Over the last four decades it too has constructed a fence between the two states, giving the lie to the idea that America needs a 'new' wall. Indeed, in many places there are already three lines of separation: occasionally a primary barrier; in urban areas, a double or secondary line of defence; and then a third fence. The US Border Patrol lists a variety of media employed in their construction.

'Primary' or most southern barriers comprise the following types:

- nothing
- three-wire cattle fence
- vertical railroad rail
- horizontal railroad rail with 6-foot drill stem uprights
- concrete filled thin-wall six-inch steel tube of staggered height
- corrugated steel plate
- perforated corrugated steel plate (landing mat)
- square tubing
- crushed cars

'Secondary' barriers comprise:

- climb-proof expanded metal fence
- climb-proof chain link fence
- concrete column or 'bollard' barrier

The map of states inherently seeks to hide from view the networks and flows of movement and energy that have always characterized human interaction and cut across the sovereign state system. When conventional, lightly manned borders fail to check the progress of population dynamics, trenches, razor wire, and breeze blocks create little more than a temporary pause in this process.

The world map includes many borders created by European empires in the 19th century and settlements after the First World War, often at the cost of defeated combatants. Part of this trend are infamous borderlines like the 1916 Sykes–Picot Agreement, which began this chapter, that defines the reach of the Syrian and Iraqi states or the 1893 Durand Line that separates contemporary Afghanistan and Pakistan. But to see borders in isolation, to view them as pure and simple demarcators of space, is to detract from the wider picture where settlements—some enduring, some temporary—provide links in chains of nodes and connections. They make up networks that enable the flow of human movement, trade, and ideas. They connect populations loosely strung across great distances. But their roles within the network feed into their meaning in their own particular, local context. As Harvard sociologist Joel Migdal observes:

> For social scientists, it is probably preferable to think of the normal state of boundaries as in flux, rather than as permanent or semi-permanent, when trying to understand the configuration of human space. To be sure, the rate of flux will vary in different circumstances. The dynamics of social life come when competing boundaries, demanding different, even contradictory practices and mental images, bump up against one another.[4]

Hence every border zone is a palimpsest on which layers of history are continually written, creating a rich, self-referential texture across the line.

During the apartheid government's civil war with the African National Congress and the South African Communist Party between the 1960s and late 1980s, South Africa's northern border with Rhodesia formed the frontline in insurgent penetration, particularly after the latter's independence. Rough, underdeveloped countryside was separated from neighbouring Rhodesia by the Limpopo River and a track that ran along it on the South African side. To this border space, apartheid governments in Pretoria attracted settler farmers. In the 1980s, they would cultivate the land and insert and root an armed defensive line against cross-border incursion by guerrilla fighters. One family, now settled on their farm, Grootplaas, had arrived via a series of settler projects. The older generation had farmed successfully in Kenya, only to move to the more favourable conditions of pre-Zimbabwe Rhodesia and then on to South Africa. Zimbabwean migrants dominate the workforce. The land is farmed by long-term employees—fixtures in this agricultural hierarchy—and transient workers who between them recalibrate the social relations. In their new home, they created between themselves a new hierarchy of status and power, and have to varying extents left Zimbabwe behind. As Maxim Bolt[5] shows, impermanence is a defining characteristic of these spaces, not only in securing employment that is scarce, unevenly formalised, yet also involves routine evasion of military and police patrols, but also in the very nature of the inversion of their professional and social status. A wave of migrants—professionals, managers, teachers, and civil servants—had been driven from their jobs following Zimbabwe's collapsed economy and repressive politics, only to arrive on the border farms. Here they find themselves in an inverse relationship to less skilled and less educated black middle managers. These less skilled workers are long-term residents on the farm from an earlier wave of migration—trusted, privileged, and empowered Zimbabweans, long embedded in the South African white owners' management structures of command and control.

But even the tenure of these locally empowered junior and middle managers is never free from the fear of personal loss of prestige and the ultimate sanction of eviction. Deeper undercurrents are at work too: 'As migrants attempt to gain a foothold in something stable, the farms themselves are far from unchanging.'[6] Cotton and citrus farms, strung like a necklace along the Limpopo River, still appear as hubs that attract migrants persistent enough to cross the river, evade the crocodiles, break through the rickety fence, and steer clear of police patrols. Closer examination shows these islands of stability tell a different story close up. The border is transient, precarious, and impermanent—even for the long-term workforce whose privilege endures by the consent of white landowners.[7] For those who stay, this particular existence is constructed out of a new set of understandings and place in the local order. Even in the post-apartheid republic, the black labour force, with apparently enduring tenure, go there but for the grace of the white owners, whose world is both local and global, at once permanent and temporary. A settler family that has farmed in Kenya, Rhodesia, and South Africa now eyes a future in a globalized world in Mozambique or beyond Africa altogether.

## No lines of separation

Populations are conditioned to treat state borders as lines of separation, fixed in time and space, that demarcate the inside world from the outside, the us from the other. States are defined by their security and tax-raising monopolies. Any behaviour that breaches those codes around their borders is illegitimate and illegal; hence cross-border smuggling should be understood as outside the law and conducted by outlaws. The truth is something different. State and substate or trans-state, and even anti-state, actors are actively complicit in each other's enterprises while outwardly conforming to the official rhetoric and trappings of sovereign government.

In the Sahel, that vast tract of the Sahara that stretches across the north of the African continent from one coast to the other, borders look different to those in Western Europe. At the same time, they are not so different from many other borders in parts of the world where geography and topography define and impede the flow of human traffic, be it as a consequence of rivers, forests, or jungles. Distance from centres of administrative power and control compounds this tendency. Geopolitics is locked into the map of empires drawn a century ago across the Middle East and North Africa. These are, however, borders which are barely lines in the sand. They are imaginary;

they exist on maps only, cutting across ethnic, language, and sectarian groups. Here are states where the remit of the monopoly of violence, centralized tax-raising powers, and the reach of national lawmaking and its enforcement are patchy, if at all present.

Natural terrain is the canvas for diverse migration patterns and movements. Even towns that appear on maps as key centres of trade and traffic offer a misleading story of the dynamics of the region. Small intersections of trade routes or water and fuel stops can be more significant in the political economy of different groups with political ambitions. North–south and east–west traditional routes represent key nodes in trans-Saharan networks of flows of people, goods, and ideas. Anthropologist Janet Roitman captures the apparent opposition between state and state challenger like this:

> emergent sub- and transnational regimes of accumulation and authority have come to dominate the Nigerian, Cameroonian, Nigérien, Chadian and Centrafrican borders. Their effective authority over certain economic activities, regional or international resources, and local populations puts them in competition with the nation-state ... while this situation seems 'oppositional', it does not necessarily imply the demise of the nation-state in the face of non-national forms of accumulation and power. ... [T]he relationships between the two realms are highly ambiguous: they are often reciprocal and complicitous as much as they are competitive and antagonistic. That is, while antagonisms are noted when it comes to the state's official regulatory authority over these regional economies, complicity is evident insofar as the state is dependent upon these regional economies for rents and the means of redistribution. Likewise, while these networks can be described as trans- or sub-national, they make important, or even essential contributions to the national political economy.[8]

A revision of how we see borders as fixed lines in space is called for. Judith Scheele has studied a settlement called al-Khalil. She calls it 'the capital of illegal trade in the northern Malian desert'.[9] It's not exactly a town, more like a truck stop. As a key node in overlapping networks, it is a locus that reveals extended power relations that lie beyond the town and are relatively independent of one another. The settlement is replete with *garājs*. Derived from the French *garage*, the word refers to dwellings, little more than courtyards capable of holding several trucks with a couple of rooms—kitchen, sleeping accommodation—and surrounded by high concrete walls and iron gates. A *garāj* is an overnight stop for trade that is just passing through. Truckers and traders are fed and stay for free, and are protected by the owner's guns. The quid pro quo is that the trader conducts his business exclusively from that *garāj* and remains loyal. From four-by-fours to camels and donkeys, a world of vehicles passes through the town. From narcotics to conflict zone weapons to all kinds of commodities, it retains a kind of Wild West flavour. But it represents so much more. Judith Scheele argues: 'Every *garāj* stands for a set of trade networks that it can draw on in times of need. These networks in turn bind local residents more closely to friends and relatives scattered throughout the Sahara on either side of the border than to their next-door neighbours.'[10] *Garājs* are nodes in a network of networks that transcends and undermines the concept of what it means to have a border. Furthermore, it defines itself in opposition to such a concept. The inhabitants of al-Khalil embody a lawlessness and statelessness. Yet at the same time they need the proximity of the Algerian state to underpin their moral economy. Without the Algerian state, roads and tracks would not be maintained, water and food infrastructure would fail. Smugglers need the state if they are to function as smugglers. And on this border, local officials are deeply implicated in cross-border activity.[11]

Networks are not new. Ghislaine Lydon underlines the importance of both literacy and the role of Islam and adherence to spoken and written Islamic law after the eighth century.[12] Mutually reinforcing developments promoted and solidified trans-Saharan trade networks. Indeed, they helped to link these routes into a wider world of trade networks that lay beyond the shores of North Africa: trade transactions recorded in writing, on paper, could bear witness to deals that had been struck and debts that would need to be honoured. Around the first century CE, long before the arrival of Islam, the camel was introduced to the Sahel. It would become the 'ship of the desert'. Because of its ability to adapt to an extreme environment, its impact on long-distance transportation of goods was dramatic. Yet more than commercial commodities were being shipped. Religious, scholarly, and ideological flows moved through these desert networks. In short, ideas and faith.[13]

Historical channels still impose an organization onto the Chad Basin, an area where Nigeria, Cameroon, Niger, Chad, and Central Africa converge. This is an area where sub- and transnational regimes of power have come to dominate local life. While this might suggest an oppositional character in a weakened and fragmenting nation state system under pressure from non-national challenge, the picture on the ground appears otherwise. Ambiguity, reciprocity, and complicity best describe the exercise of authority and pursuit of accumulation in this space.[14] Along the Chad and Cameroon border, the state declares little border traffic illegal. Military officers regularly switch back and forth from acting as customs officials. They supplement their inadequate salaries that trickle from central state coffers, thus benefiting the overall state. But this only scratches the surface of this economy.

For states, like Niger and Chad, whose currencies are non-convertible in currency markets, the state plays an active part in trading in illegal goods and contravening its own laws. So in Niger the state takes the lead in trading in illegal American cigarettes in order to generate foreign currency. This state-sanctioned, otherwise illegal trade fits into wider networks across the Sahel:

> In this instance, state actors collude with, and are dependent upon, intermediaries (e.g. Tuareg) who control certain trade routes and are notorious for providing security in dangerous zones (such as the south of Algeria and the Niger-Chad border) not only for personal profit, but also to respond to the insolvency of the state and its associated political risks (e.g. the demands of unpaid state bureaucrats, including police and *gens d'armes*).[15]

Layered over the Chad Basin, simultaneously undermining the idea of sovereign nation states while underpinning their continued existence, is a security map. Conceived through the hegemonic eyes of Western politico-military cartographers, this map tells the story of a world filled with complexity, uncertainty, and turbulence. On this map, cross-border networks, both historic and newly globalized, disappear. And so too do the tracks of a thousand years drawn in the sand.

It is this map which underpins French counterterrorism forces' interventions in Mali. Their mission was to combat Salafi jihadi fighters who had seized the north of the country. What the overarching Western story of global jihad obscured then and now in Mali is an account of historical instability rooted in a sovereign state that at best has always struggled to function according to most criteria of what it means to be a state, whose extended borders are porous on their many sides, and which barely behaves as a state applying conventional norms of the European state map.

Mali is bordered by seven other states: Algeria, Mauritania, Senegal, Guinea, Côte d'Ivoire, Burkina Faso, and Niger. Sovereign reach of the central state is variable in each of these countries. Mali is no different. It is, like many of its neighbours, a hollowed-out state where the outer bureaucratic and administrative shell seems to be in place but where state assets have been emptied out to the benefit of political elites and vested interests. New 'fast money' commodities like narcotics (as opposed to traditional cigarette or petrol smuggling) have mapped onto historic trans-Saharan networks of trade routes that connect population centres. These settlements were originally established by Muslim Sufi saints who travelled across the northern half of the continent.

The Greek writer Herodotus in his *Histories* in the 5th century BCE talks of the Garamantes, a tribal people living in the southern deserts of what today we call Libya: 'to the south of this region … that is teeming with wild animals, are the Garamantes who shun all human intercourse and contact'.[16] The tribe Herodotus observed we know today as the Tuareg or Kel Tamasheq. The story of post-1960s Tuareg separatism in the post-independence states of Mali and Niger enhances our discussion of borders. And, in turn, that account is informed by Tuareg's highly structured clan system. At the same time, Malian politics is affected by a growing black versus white—that is, dark versus light-skinned—racial dimension. This often reflects and is processed through historical and continued ownership of slaves. Trade in human commodities locks into regional trafficking routes that transport and sell women for the sex trade and children for labour. And Mali's story is even further complicated by a wave of diverse, reformist, Salafi Islamist groups that has threatened the state and fuelled concern of western states, particularly European countries with their vulnerable North African diaspora populations.

Taken together with other dimensions that make up Mali's recent history, a picture emerges that is removed from the simplistic view propagated in Washington and Westminster, and by Western media. It is not that the presence of political Islam replaces these other factors. Rather, it informs them and is deeply implicated in them. It grows out of and blends into deeper underlying causes. At the heart of a series of mutating insurgencies is Tuareg's secessionist militancy. Their claims to their own state identity date back to Mali's independence from France in June 1960. Between 1962 and 1964, the largely nomadic Tuaregs resisted enforced incorporation into the postcolonial state and pursued their aim of creating their own Tuareg state of Azawad. The first Tuareg rebellion was followed by a second between 1990 and 1996 and a third between 2007 and 2009. Then 2012 saw the fourth uprising by the Tuaregs since independence. What this simple trajectory obscures is central government's use of 'militiatary' strategy. This was the deliberate stirring up of inter- and intra-racial rivalries in the north (historically Tuareg country) through the use of private and rival ethnic Arab militias under the control of cigarette and arms smugglers.[17]

In its most recent manifestation, the latest uprising forms part of an ever-mutating but triangular struggle between the three forces of (i) successively weak Malian governments; (ii) Tuareg secessionists; and (iii) Salafi jihadi fighters. Sometimes Tuaregs serve as soldiers in the Malian armed forces before choosing to revolt and fight against them. Sometimes Tuaregs—who remain intent on declaring independence—link up with the militant Islamists—who prefer the spiritual-legal domain associated with sharia to actual independence identified with secular statehood—only for Tuaregs to break with and fight the same militant Islamists later.

Meanwhile al-Qaeda in the Islamic Maghreb (AQIM) has since 2007 secured a sanctuary inside northern Mali and operated as a state within a state, levying taxes, administering justice, and providing policing. The Movement for Unity and Jihad in West Africa—MUJAO and Ansar Dine (both splinter groups of AQIM), Libya's Ansar al-Sharia, and occasionally Nigeria's Boko Haram contest the north of the country with Tuareg movements such as the Azawad National Liberation Movement—MNLA the Arab Movement of Azawad—MAA, the Coordination of Movements of Azawad—CMA, and the Islamic Movement of Azawad—MIA. Scholar Stephen Harmon suggests: 'The Islamist militias, with logistical and material support based on marriage alliances and recruitment of local youths, were able to, after seemingly coming out of nowhere, turn the tables on their one time rebel associates the [Tuareg] MNLA and take control of the northern cities themselves.'[18] For all that this is a story of the Malian central government's loss of control and legitimacy, it is also one of the sustained knock-on effects from neighbouring Algerian politics. An explosion of social movements that grew out of trade unionists, feminists, Berber ethnic campaigners, journalists, and students helped bring about Algeria's dramatic election result in June 1990. Local and regional elections led to the Islamic Salvation Front (FIS) winning control over half of the municipal bodies in the country. The following year, in December 1991, the elections produced an even more dramatic result. The FIS secured 188 seats out of a total of 232 in Round 1 of the country's first-ever democratic elections.

Humiliation followed for the FLN (Front de Libération Nationale) government, which had retained power since 1961 following its independence war with France. This shock result led to the imposition of martial law and imprisonment of the FIS leadership. Significantly, an uncompromising counterterror campaign was launched against Islamic fundamentalists, who were pursued throughout Algeria. Reports suggest that 150,000 people were killed and 6,000 disappeared in what has been described as the 'dirty war'. Many supporters of the FIS would go on to embrace Islamic political militancy.

In short, in Algeria the 1990s proved to be a decade of atrocities and massacres committed by state forces and Islamic insurgents (the Armed Islamic Group—GIA). The effect was to see breakaway Islamists create the Salafist Group for Preaching and Combat (GSPC) and, subsequently, the AQIM. Many of those militants would be driven south by unremitting counterterror campaigns into the sparse and marginalized populations and terrain of northern Mali, where they allied with other resistance groups.

Mali's is also a story of the local fallout from Colonel Muammar al-Gaddafi's demise in Libya in October 2011. The collapse of the Libyan state and the fragmenting of the country from early 2012 marked the return to Mali of heavily armed Tuaregs who had been formerly employed in Gaddafi's army, but suddenly found themselves jobless.[19] Mali's Islamic fundamentalist progression is thus not as simple as it first appears. Rather, it speaks to a local history of black African and Arab groups competing inside Mali, as well as subordinate groups contesting power with dominant castes within a strict, Tuareg, hierarchical clan system. Meanwhile the region's politics and economies play out in a way that is at odds with the imperial map drawn by the European powers a century ago. Here regional politics conform to historical and traditional as well as ecological, economic and spiritual flows that intersect and network the contemporary Malian state.

## Maps to Paradise

The same dynamics play out in conflict theatres that hold a tight grip on Syria and Iraq, where the Sykes–Picot Agreement that carved up the terrain of the post-Ottoman Middle East recently passed its centenary. Sykes–Picot has a certain primacy in the mythology of the Islamic State. Historian Max Hastings cites two videos from the militant organization, released on the day in 2014 when the Islamic State (ISIS/ISIL/Daesh) announced itself to the world as the Islamic caliphate. In one, a gunman addresses his audience with the sentiment: 'This is the so-called Sykes-Picot. We don't recognize it, and we will never recognize it. Inshallah, we break other borders also, but we start with this one, inshallah.'[20] Hastings goes on to quote a Turkish historian who argues that Islamic State's fixation on the 1916 event distorts not just their own but other actors' understandings too: 1916 is 'feeding people's own narratives of themselves as playthings of outsiders'. And this view is backed up by another historian, Sean McMeekin, who reminds us of the secondary involvement of the two diplomats in drawing up the infamous map, instead highlighting the lead taken by the Soviet foreign minister Sergei Sazonov: 'None of the most notorious post-Ottoman borders—those separating Palestine from Jordan, or Syria from Iraq, or Iraq from Kuwait—were drawn by Sykes and Picot. Even the boundaries they did sketch out ... were jettisoned after the war.'[21]

Ambiguity shrouds any reading of borders clinically and authoritatively captured on modern maps. Cross-border dynamics mean every attempt at mapping reflects some variety of endogenous ambition and interest. Fences, no matter how high or long, cannot keep the lines on the map. The will to carve the lines of our maps into stone and metal simply reflects the utopian role of mapping in history.

Scafi notes that in the Middle Ages the belief was widespread that 'Paradise was a real place on Earth' and could be found on maps. This conflicted with geographic fact. Medieval cartographers had to create a 'visual language' to manage this paradox and make Paradise real.[22] Practical maps, for traversing specific place and space, had no need for Paradise. But the map of a complete world must include the problem of time in the medieval world—namely, the Fall, implied by the representation of Paradise. Maps combined 'early geography and the spiritual history of the Christian world'.[23] No wonder that as the Renaissance emerged, Paradise was relegated to a separate 'inaccessible' space, a non-place on the corner of the sheet adjacent to geographical drawings. In time, as the *mappa mundi* declined as a mode of cartography,

Paradise disappeared from maps altogether. 'The loss of Paradise from world maps was no insignificant cartographic omission. It represents a major shift in thought as well as in mapping. The space-time vision of medieval times was broken ... the notion of a geography inextricably linked to the whole space-time structure was lost.'[24] That loss of unity of the spatial and temporal is seen as integral to the rise of the modern era, and it leaves a legacy in the contemporary desire for its recovery through new forms of mapping. Apollo 8 mission commander Frank Borman echoes Stewart Brand: 'When you're finally up on the moon looking back at Earth, all those differences and nationalistic traits are pretty well going to blend and you're going to get a concept that maybe this is one world and why the hell can't we learn to live together like decent people.'[25] This is the alternative hope attached to taking the lines off the map of the world and seeking its utopian replacement by a universal network of individuals.

Maps, especially those of nation state borders, are today increasingly fetishized.[26] But their unravelling into networks can be fetishized too. Our faith in maps, both vertical or horizontal, mask the ways in which the intersection between different cartographic assumptions determines what any line really signifies: 'We must be attentive to the ways in which our maps act on the world and circulate throughout the world, and whether or not our maps are even composed in ways that are conducive to producing the sort of change we aim for.'[27] Maps always fulfil different purposes. Maps do not represent lines, they generate them so that they act in the world. Faith in mapping, and the borders we may draw in space, expresses a desire to make sense of the world that haunts all historiography. There is no salvation to be found in state maps and their clear lines. Uncertainties and challenges that orientate the world today were written into existence by the ways in which networks and hierarchies meshed together to form the lines of the 21st century. The future is continually redrawn like windswept lines that vanish in the sand.

# Conclusion

The history of the present is not one of globalization of the state form from a single European location. Nor is it simply a story about the rise of the network that displaces and replaces the state as a principle of global order. It is a history of termite-like negotiations between networks and hierarchies, of proxy wars and local struggles, settling and resettling the accounts between these two opposed maps. As religious networks gave rise to the modern state in Europe, so too did states nurture networks and give rise to global empires. Which in turn folded back into the state map.[1] Each micro-negotiation between state and network had to be written out of our maps for history to be given direction and sense. To recognize that networks of adventurers and chartered companies carved out a world that collapsed into state lines found on our maps today, just as the swarming armies of the Mongols collapsed into rigid territories, is to accept their historical contingency but not necessarily the fragility of the maps they left behind.[2] To recognize that every network carries within it hierarchies of various kinds should not lead us to forget that the map of horizontal networks has been at work, often in the form of the feared opponent of the state, in every historical event or process, every social or political organization.

It is the function of mapping to shape material realities. In this book, we have argued that history is a process of negotiation between centralizing and decentralizing forces at the intersection of two maps: the map of the state and the map of the network. By necessity, our choice of cases may appear idiosyncratic. Our point is that their dynamic interaction is timeless. The wide sweep of our endeavour in sampling from across world history has, we hope, been illuminating; but it also reinforces this central point. Representation is central to the formation of the world we inhabit today. In this sense, mapping is productive of space. But this is not simply invention or a process of imagination. As we spread our faulty maps across world history, we are doing more than hiding the facts on the ground. More than obscuring the world, map-makers are in the business of seeking to resolve the background tension between the state and network that is at work in every historical form, social movement, bureaucracy, insurgency, and institution.

This book is written in a form that seeks to reflect the central point we hoped to make: that the interaction between networks and hierarchies is a constant in history. The theoretical architecture that roots this argument echoes the work of French philosophers Gilles Deleuze and Felix Guattari. That this is implicit is no accident. Rather it reflects an approach to reading and working they too advocated: to take forward ideas and set them on a new trajectory; and, most important, to put concepts to work and find their value in what they make possible.

It is nonetheless worth making some general comments regarding what is at stake in the theoretical moves we have made here and in relationship to the broader conceptual framework that underpins the book. The world is no more, no less complex than it ever has been. This book's structure reflects the historical ontology behind our argument. History does not possess inherent tendencies. This is why making sense of the present and the past requires a recognition that our mappings are at the centre of creating all events, processes and histories. Exploring how vertical and horizontal maps interplay is the only way to make sense of our present. This book makes the case for applying its thinking to various matters of concern like terrorism, migration, climate change, and pandemics. Moreover, to strategic technological and social challenges of the 21st century.

The coronavirus pandemic continues to sweep the globe in the early 21st century. And it reinforces the significance of these two maps. The relationship between mapping as a representational device (identifying challenges like the pandemic) and mapping as an organizing or governance practice (responding to it as a crisis) is central to what our book has sought to achieve. The state map and network map are deployed by diverse actors in world politics, from militaries to governments, social movements, insurgents, and transnational, religious diasporas. Politics across these spaces forms in the space between our representations; it's where actions occur in the world.

The epistemological and ontological implications of our argument are rooted in the difficulty of imagining the present. Whether we reflect on social disorder, climate change, or the future of the nation state, the problem is the same. To create knowledge is to recognize that no actual historical form is a perfect expression of tendencies we may see at work. Neither network nor state ever appears as itself. To see world history this way is to see the world anew. It is to identify the mechanics of how our representations weave the world into its shape.

Explaining post-structuralist ontological and epistemological claims in an accessible way, as we have attempted here, is a delicate undertaking. It requires drawing out the relationship between our mental images or maps and real things we see in the world that include hierarchical and horizontal logics at work simultaneously. We hope to have captured the interplay between representations and processes of assemblage to see what mapping and unmapping can do. Mapping misleads, and unmapping illuminates. In this sense, this book is an attempt to sustain this different way of thinking and show how it can function in practice. Unmapping, as we understand it, requires more than simply recognizing that we all have a tendency to oversimplification or overcredulity with respect to our cherished assumptions about the world. Our point is not only that everyone needs to think carefully about the maps they use. The relationship between the state map of verticality and the network map of horizontality shapes real-world politics today. And it always has.

Our purpose in this book was to show that theory is not something disconnected from the world. It makes possible and shapes the 21st century. Our maps are bound up with material relations that our representations are reaching for. They speak of the future and how to remake it. Principally, however, we hope our central argument lands with you the reader: only by unmapping the 21st century can we imagine its future, revealing the relationship between cognitive maps as part and parcel of everything represented. The world makes claims on us. To unmap is to acknowledge those claims, to pull apart what vertical and horizontal processes, state and network maps, do to shape the reality we see. We continually seek and fail to grasp that interaction with our maps. The hope of this book has been no more, no less than to make this simple point.

# Afterword

Gilles Deleuze and Félix Guattari's work provides a cumbersome and, at first glance, intimidating conceptual toolbox. Their approach to thought and intellectual endeavour is centred on the idea that philosophers are obliged to experiment by creating new concepts and, when inspired by others, set their ideas onto unexpected, nonetheless revealing, trajectories. How effectively we have done so in this book, our readers will determine. But this afterword sets out the rationale behind the conceptual moves we have made.

The maps discussed in this book reflect what the philosophers Deleuze and Guattari referred to as 'virtual diagrams'. Writing in *A Thousand Plateaus*, diagrams are what they term 'real' abstractions.[1] This is to say, they are tools of interpretation which reflect material tendencies in the world. To make sense of that world requires untangling the logics that govern our representations, from a world that has its own intensities and directions that carve out the space for those representations. The philosophers agree with the commonly expressed idea that our impressions of the world have only a complicated connection with the world itself. We reach out into the world and find patterns of abstraction already working within it, they argue. These abstractions or virtual diagrams, then, are not simply imagined. They constrain and inform how we interpret what we see and, consequently, what we do. Our intellectual tools are traps for understanding. But this does not mean the diagrams by which we make sense of things do not somehow reflect rules of organization that emerge out of the fabric of the material world itself. We are directed in forming our thoughts by the abstract tendencies present in what we experience.

When Deleuze and Guattari argue that the state is a virtual diagram, they mean it is not just a thing out there. Rather, the state is a set of abstract rules that govern our interpretations. What they highlight is that when we try to make sense of the world, it always involves searching for some kind of ideal. This 'ideal state' provides the conditions that allow us to recognize states as states in the present or past. Similarly, when they talk of 'nomadism' as a virtual diagram, they are saying that nomadic societies carry within them a recognizable tendency, even if they don't perfectly align to that ideal in practice: actual nomads follow the seasons when they move between pastures.

Deleuze and Guattari suggest that what we see in the world only makes sense through shortcuts by which we simplify and categorize. Our heuristics may well lead us astray. But applying those ideals reflects something to be found in the thing we are talking about that also tends in the direction of those ideals we have in mind. The challenge of paralleling Deleuze and Guattari's work is to make a more accessible or user-friendly toolbox. The central arguments they put forward are intuitive but extremely challenging. They were trying to cast fresh light on a perennial problem in philosophy, one going back to Plato: we define things (processes, events, movements, actors) by what they are not entirely, but almost are, or might be a little.

Their point is materialist in a formal sense. Abstractions they identify form the conditions of possibility for bodies, actors, institutions, and processes that make up the world. Yet the structures themselves do no work outside the role they play as heuristics to manage our perceptions. The state map and the network map, in this sense, are not 'out there'. Rather, they reflect ideals within that world that organize it, make it sensible, and allow us to grasp it. These abstractions sit in every form, event, or body, defining what it can do (its body 'without organs', as they put it), yet without any body, form, or event actually taking that pure shape. This is why Deleuze and Guattari are called post-structuralists. The ideal structures they describe are not actually there. They are potentials, not things, which make possible our interpretations of the world, but also inevitably frustrate them.

Deleuze and Guattari talk about the process by which abstract diagrams (or maps) take shape in the world as a process of assemblage. All assemblages in the world (a state, social movement, bureaucracy, institution, or corporation) exist for us as diagrams that make sense. Actual assemblages in the world are mixed, and only make sense if we see them as multiple diagrams assembling together. This observation underpins the central point throughout this book: networks and hierarchies are always folded together and assembled. They involve people's interpretations in the process of how they take shape in the world.

*Unmapping the 21st Century* uses the concept of mapping to capture virtual diagrams and their relationship to assemblages. For Deleuze and Guattari, there are two principal abstract diagrams. One is made up of 'molar lines', structured as a pyramid, a tree, under a vertical system of striation. The other is made up of 'molecular lines', structured like a rhizome (a natural root structure) under a horizontal system of striation. We call these 'maps': the map of state and map of network. State and network maps capture abstract tendencies present in matter itself, but also the means for recognizing those tendencies. Our maps of the present are not the world; they simply capture the contradictory heuristics at work in its formation.

An intricacy in Deleuze and Guattari's argument is the 'line of flight'. This concept is often misread as expressing freedom, revolution, and creativity writ large. But they had something more prosaic in mind. They mean that actual assemblages exist in time as well as space. Whether we are talking about social movements, physical objects, or institutions, each is caught in temporal motion. In other words, they see the role of change, transformation, movement, and development in every assemblage. So virtual diagrams are always assembled *in time*.

Assemblage is the process of connecting diagrams at specific times and in specific spaces. Line of flight observes that the spatial world we inhabit exists on a trajectory. To make sense of space requires making sense of how assemblages link different logics, modes, and ideals in time. The line of flight is not good, nor liberating, nor necessarily positive. It is simply time, expressed through the assemblage of abstract diagrams in every historical formation.

The line of flight, understood as the temporal process of assemblage, is what we have referred to in this book as unmapping. This theoretical move away from Deleuze and Guattari's terminology is, we believe, clearer about what is principally at stake. The object of unmapping is to make sense of how things are assembled without assuming any internal direction. Unmapping involves reading every assemblage as a particular moment in history. There is no inevitability to how state and network take shape together. Our weaving together diverse attempts to map them seeks to illuminate how the 21st century is being made—to a great extent, chaotically and contingently everywhere. This is, we believe, a question of unmapping.

Much like belief in the state's inevitability—a not uncommon conviction—is belief in networks' inevitable victory over the state. Each assumes maps carry within them the secret or hidden truth of history and social order. No wonder the return of the state is surprising. We do not claim the world is *increasingly* riven by complexity and networked, let alone fated to return to a world of states. Our argument is that the future of both state and network depends on how they interact in local and contingent moves. Neither quite makes sense of the future. But observing conversations across time illuminates possible patterns for all strategists, politicians, and revolutionaries.

# Notes

## Introduction

1  Michael Cox, *The Post-Cold War World: Turbulence and Change in World Politics Since the Fall*, London: Routledge, 2018. Jean G. Boulton, Peter M. Allen, and Cliff Bowman, *Embracing Complexity: Strategic Perspectives for an Age of Turbulence*, Oxford: Oxford University Press, 2015. Alan Greenspan, *The Age of Turbulence: Adventures in a New World*, London: Penguin, 2008.

2  James N. Rosenau, *Distant Proximities: Dynamics beyond Globalization*, Princeton, NJ: Princeton University Press, 2003; p 11.

3  Rosenau, *Distant Proximities*; p 12. See Tim Stevens and Nicholas Michelsen, eds, *Pessimism in International Relations: Provocations, Possibilities, Politics*, Cham: Springer, 2019.

4  Joshua Keating, *Invisible Countries: Journeys to the Edge of Nationhood*, New Haven, CT: Yale University Press, 2018.

5  Janet Abrams and Peter Hall, eds, *Else/Where: Mapping New Cartographies of Networks and Territories*, Minneapolis: University of Minnesota Press, 2006.

6  Denis Cosgrove, 'Introduction: mapping meaning', in Denis Cosgrove, ed, *Mappings*, London: Reaktion Books, 1999, pp 1–23; pp 4–5. Kennan Ferguson, 'Unmapping and remapping the world', in Michael J. Shapiro and Hayward R. Alker, eds, *Challenging Boundaries: Global Flows, Territorial Identities*, Borderlines Volume 2, Minneapolis: University of Minnesota Press, 1996; p 165, p 170.

7  J. B. Harley, *The New Nature of Maps: Essays in the History of Cartography*, Baltimore: Johns Hopkins.

8  Sankaran Krishna, 'Cartographic anxiety'; p 209.

9  Yuliya Komska 'Introduction: a discontiguous Eastern Europe', in Irene Kacandes and Yuliya Komska, eds, *Eastern Europe Unmapped: Beyond Borders and Peripheries*, New York: Berghahn Books, 2017, pp 1–28; p 4.

10  Levi R. Bryant, *Onto-cartography: an Ontology of Machines and Media*, Edinburgh: Edinburgh University Press, 2014.

11  David Chandler, *Ontopolitics in the Anthropocene: an Introduction to Mapping, Sensing and Hacking*, Abingdon: Routledge, 2018.

12  Manuel De Landa, *A Thousand Years of Nonlinear History*, Princeton, NJ: Princeton University Press, 2021.

13  Ferguson, 'Unmapping and remapping the world'; p 165.

14  Alberto Toscano and Jeff Kinkle, *Cartographies of the Absolute*, Lanham, MD: John Hunt Publishing, 2015; p 19, p 24.

15  Toscano and Kinkle, *Cartographies of the Absolute*; p 4.

16  Komska 'Introduction: a discontiguous Eastern Europe'; p 2.

17  Manuel Castells, *The Rise of the Network Society*, Chichester: Wiley-Blackwell, 2011.

[18] Benjamin H. Bratton, Nicolay Boyadjiev, and Nick Axel, eds, *The New Normal*, Zurich: Park Books, 2020; p 61.

[19] Bratton, Boyadjiev, and Axel, *The New Normal*; p 18. Manuel De Landa, *Assemblage Theory*, Edinburgh: Edinburgh University Press, 2016.

[20] David M. Berry and Alexander R. Galloway, 'A network is a network is a network: reflections on the computational and the societies of control', *Theory, Culture & Society* 33 (4) 2016: 151–72; p 160.

[21] Amitav Ghosh, *The Great Derangement: Climate Change and the Unthinkable*, Chicago: University of Chicago Press, 2016.

[22] Walter Benjamin, *Illuminations: Essays and Reflections*, New York: Random House, 1968.

[23] As is laid out in the Afterword, in developing this concept of unmapping, we are building on the collected writings of Gilles Deleuze and Félix Guattari, especially *A Thousand Plateaus: Capitalism and Schizophrenia*, London: Bloomsbury, 1988. Please see Manuel De Landa's *Intensive Science and Virtual Philosophy*, New York: Bloomsbury, 2013, for a materialist reading which we found insightful and helpful.

## Chapter 1

[1] J. B. Harley, 'Deconstructing the map', in Trevor J. Barnes and J. S. Duncan, eds, *Writing Worlds: Discourse, Text and Metaphor in the Representation of Landscape*, London: Routledge, 1992, pp 231–47; p 244.

[2] Peter Barber and Tom Harper, *Magnificent Maps: Power, Propaganda and Art*, London: British Library, 2010; p 81.

[3] Barber and Harper, *Magnificent Maps*.

[4] Henri Lefebvre, 'Space and the state', in Neil Brenner, Bob Jessop, Martin Jones, and Gordon Macleod, eds, *State/Space: a Reader*, Malden, MA: Blackwell Publishing, 2003, pp 84–100; p 84.

[5] Lefebvre, 'Space and the state'; p 84.

[6] Lefebvre, 'Space and the state'; p 84.

[7] Lefebvre, 'Space and the state'; p 85.

[8] Neil Smith, *American Empire: Roosevelt's Geographer and the Prelude to Globalization*, Berkeley: University of California Press, 2004, pp 92–6.

[9] Daniel Woolf, *The Social Circulation of the Past, English Historical Culture 1500–1730*, Oxford: Oxford University Press, 2003; p 304.

[10] Scott Anderson, *Lawrence in Arabia*, London: Atlantic Books, 2013; p 162.

[11] Paul Virilio, *Speed and Politics: an Essay on Dromology*, translated by Mark Polizzotti, Los Angeles: Semiotext(e), 2006; p 133.

[12] Cited in Nicholas Papayanis, *Planning Paris before Haussmann*, Baltimore: Johns Hopkins University Press, 2004; p 19.

[13] David Jordan, *Transforming Paris*, New York: The Free Press, 1995; p 187.

[14] Papayanis, *Planning Paris before Haussmann*.

[15] Jordan, *Transforming Paris*; p 192.

[16] Cited in Virilio, *Speed and Politics*; p 29.

[17] Leif Jerram, *Streetlife*, Oxford: Oxofrd University Press, 2011; p 49.

[18] David Harvey, *Rebel Cities*, London: Verso, 2012; p xvii.

[19] Aristide Zolberg, 'Moments of madness', *Politics & Society*, 2 (2) 1972: 183–207.

[20] Jerram, *Streetlife*; p 35.

[21] Okun Semen, *Putilovets v trekh revolyutsiyakh: sbornik materialov po istorii Putilovskogo zavoda* [Putilovets in Three Revolutions: A Collection of Materials on the History of the Putilov Factory], History of Plants, Moscow-Leningrad: OGIZ State Publishing House, 1933, pp 309–441.

22  S. A. Smith, *Red Petrograd: Revolution in the Factories 1917–18*, Cambridge: Cambridge University Press, 1983; p 8.

23  Mikhail Baryshnikov, 'V. P. Baranovskiy. Chastnaya initsiativa v oboronnom sektore rossiyskoy ekonomiki nachala XX veka' [V. P. Baranovsky. Private initiative in the defense sector of the Russian economy in the beginning of the 20th century], *Vestnik SPbGU: Seriya 8. Menedzhment* [St Petersburg State University Bulletin: Series 8. Management], Issue 3, 2016: 139–65.

24  Jerram, *Streetlife*; p 36.

25  Eyal Weizman, 'Urban warfare: walking through walls', in *Hollow Land: Israel's Architecture of Occupation*, London: Verso, 2007, pp 185–220; p 195.

26  Eyal Weizman, 'Urban warfare: walking through walls', in *Hollow Land: Israel's Architecture of Occupation*, London: Verso, 2007, pp 185–220; p 195.

27  Weizman, 'Urban Warfare'; pp 185–8.

## Chapter 2

1   Anna Lowenhaupt Tsing, *The Mushroom at the End of the World: On the Possibility of Life in Capitalist Ruins*, Princeton, NJ: Princeton University Press, 2015.

2   Timothy Morton, *Dark Ecology: For a Logic of Future Coexistence*, New York: Columbia University Press, 2016.

3   Frank McLynn, *Genghis Khan: The Man who Conquered the World*, London: Bodley Head, 2015; p 493.

4   Joseph Fletcher, 'The Mongols: ecological and social perspectives', *Harvard Journal of Asiatic Studies*, 46 (1) 1986: 11–50; p 33.

5   Gareth Jenkins, 'A note on climatic cycles and the rise of Chinggis Khan', *Central Asiatic Journal*, 18 (4) 1974: 217–26.

6   Neil Pederson, Amy E. Hessl, Nachin Baatarbileg, Kevin J. Anchukaitis, and Nicola Di Cosmo, 'Pluvials, droughts, the Mongol Empire, and modern Mongolia', *Proceedings of the National Academy of Sciences*, 111 (12) 2014: 4375–9.

7   Marie Favereau, *The Horde: How the Mongols Changed the World*, Cambridge, MA: Belknap Press, 2021; p 2.

8   Favereau, *The Horde*.

9   McLynn, *Genghis Khan*; p 127.

10  McLynn, *Genghis Khan*; p 105.

11  McLynn, *Genghis Khan*; p 505.

12  Ibn Khaldûn, *The Muqaddimah: An Introduction to History*, three volumes, Princeton, NJ: Princeton University Press, 1969.

13  Deleuze and Guattari, *A Thousand Plateaus*.

14  Pierre Clastres, *Society against the State: Essays in Political Anthropology*, Princeton, NJ: Princeton University Press, 2020.

15  Deleuze and Guattari, *A Thousand Plateaus*.

16  Deleuze and Guattari, *A Thousand Plateaus*.

17  C. Clauswitz, *On War*, Princeton, NJ: Princeton, 1984.

18  Stephen D. Krasner, 'Compromising Westphalia', *International Security*, 20 (3) 1995: 115–51.

19  Hannah Arendt, *On Revolution*, London: Penguin Classics, 2006.

20  Filippo Tommaso Marinetti, 'The futurist manifesto', *Le Figaro*, 20 February 1909: 39–44.

21  Jens Steffek, 'Fascist internationalism', *Millennium* 44 (1) 2015: 3–22.

22  Walter Benjamin, *The Work of Art in the Age of Mechanical Reproduction*, London: Penguin, 2008. Benjamin, *Illuminations*.

23  Benjamin, *Illuminations*.

24  Benjamin, *Illuminations.*
25  Mikael Bakunin, *The Reaction in Germany,* 1842. https://theanarchistlibrary.org/library, accessed 8 April 2022.
26  John Strachey, *The Menace of Fascism,* London: Victor Gollancz, 1933.
27  Helmut Thielicke, *Nihilism: Its Origin and Nature—with a Christian Answer,* New York: Harper, 1961.
28  Gilles Deleuze and Félix Guattari, *Anti-Oedipus: Capitalism and Schizophrenia,* Minneapolis: University of Minnesota Press, 1983.
29  Zygmunt Bauman, *Modernity and the Holocaust,* Ithaca, NY: Cornell University Press, 1989.
30  Andrew Culp, *Dark Deleuze,* Minneapolis: University of Minnesota Press, 2016, p 55.
31  Daniel Siemens, *Stormtroopers: A New History of Hitler's Brownshirts,* New Haven, CT: Yale University Press, 2017.
32  Roger Griffin, 'Revolution from the right: fascism', in David Parker, ed, *Revolutions and the Revolutionary Tradition in the West 1560–1991,* 2000, pp 185–201.
33  Jason Campbell Sharman, *Empires of the Weak,* Princeton, NJ: Princeton University Press, 2019.

## Chapter 3

1   Bruce Chatwin, *The Songlines,* London: Vintage, 1988; p 2.
2   Cited in Danièle Klapproth, *Narrative as Social Practice: Anglo-Western and Australian Aboriginal Oral Traditions,* Berlin: Mouton de Gruyter, 2004, pp 68–9.
3   Diana Eades, 'You gotta know how to talk ...: information seeking in South-East Queensland Aboriginal Society', *Australian Journal of Linguistics,* 2 (1), 1982: 61–82.
4   Ronald Berndt, *Australian Aboriginal Religion,* Leiden: E. J. Brill, 1974, p 8.
5   Chatwin, *The Songlines,* p 13.
6   Elizabeth A. Povinelli, *Geontologies: A Requiem to Late Liberalism,* Durham, NC: Duke University Press, 2016.
7   Robert Hughes, *The Fatal Shore,* London: Vintage, 2003, p 1.
8   Hughes, *The Fatal Shore;* p 17.
9   Thomas Hobbes, *Leviathan,* Harmondsworth: Penguin, 1971.
10  John Locke, *Second Treatise of Government,* edited by Crawford B. Macpherson, Indianapolis: Hackett, 1980.
11  Lewis Hyde, *Common As Air,* London: Union Books, 2012; p 31.
12  Roger Kain, John Chapman, and Richard Oliver, *The Enclosure Maps of England and Wales 1595–1918,* Cambridge: Cambridge University Press, 2004; p 1.
13  Christopher Hill, *The World Turned Upside Down,* London: Penguin, 1991; p 39.
14  Hill, *The World Turned Upside Down;* pp 40–1.
15  E. P. Thompson, *The Making of the English Working Class,* London: Victor Gollancz, 1963; p 218.
16  Bryony McDonagh, 'Negotiating enclosure in sixteenth-century Yorkshire: the South Cave Dispute, 1530–1536', in Jane Whittle, ed, *Landlords and Tenants in Britain: Tawney's Agrarian Problem Revisited,* Woodbridge: The Boydell Press, 2013, pp 52–66; p 53.
17  Jairus Banaji, *A Brief History of Commercial Capitalism,* Chicago: Haymarket Books, 2020; p 26.
18  Banaji, *A Brief History of Commercial Capitalism;* p 47.
19  'Capitalism only Triumphs when it becomes identified with the State, when it is the state' (Fernand Braudel, quoted in Banaji, *A Brief History of Commercial Capitalism;* p 133).
20  Peter Linebaugh and Marcus Rideker, *The Many-headed Hydra,* Boston: Beacon Press, 2013; pp 49–50.
21  Linebaugh and Rideker, *The Many-headed Hydra;* pp 50–1.

22 Linebaugh and Rideker, *The Many-headed Hydra*; p 56.

23 Linebaugh and Rideker, *The Many-headed Hydra*; p 59.

24 Linebaugh and Rideker, *The Many-headed Hydra*; p 110.

25 Karl Polanyi, *The Great Transformation*, Boston: Beacon Press, 2001; p 84.

26 Linebaugh and Rideker, *The Many-headed Hydra*; p 145.

27 Kathryn Cullen-DuPont, *Human Trafficking*, New York: Infobase Publishing, 2009; p 6.

28 Ronald Segal, *Islam's Black Slaves*, London: Atlantic Books, 2001; p 102.

29 David McNally, *Blood and Money: War, Slavery, Finance, and Empire*, Chicago: Haymarket Books, 2020; p 5.

30 Rebecca Shumway, *The Fante and the Transatlantic Slave Trade*, Rochester: University of Rochester Press, 2011; pp 33–4.

31 McNally, *Blood and Money*; p 50.

32 McNally, *Blood and Money*; p 76.

33 Cyril Lionel Robert James, *The Black Jacobins: Toussaint L'Ouverture and the San Domingo Revolution*, London: Penguin, 2001.

34 Linebaugh and Rideker, *The Many-headed Hydra*; p 157.

35 Sylvia Wynter, 'Novel and history, plot and plantation', *Savacou*, 5, 1971: 95–102. See discussion in Aaron Kamugisha, *Beyond Coloniality: Citizenship and Freedom in the Caribbean Intellectual Tradition*, Blooomington: Indiana University Press, 2019.

36 Thomas Kidd, *The Great Awakening*, New Haven, CT: Yale University Press, 2007; p 12.

37 Brett Rushforth and Paul W. Mapp, *Colonial North America and the Atlantic World*, London and New York: Routledge, 2009; pp 269–270

38 Letter, 17 April 1741, *The Pennsylvania Gazette*, No 592, p 1, http://cdm15933.conten tdm.oclc.org/cdm/ref/collection/p15933coll3/id/80 [sic], accessed 24 July 2015.

39 Peter Charles Hoffer, *The Great New York Conspiracy*, Lawrence, KS: University Press of Kansas, 2003; p 3.

40 Hoffer, *The Great New York Conspiracy*; p 168.

41 Hoffer, *The Great New York Conspiracy*; p 174.

42 David Featherstone, *Resistance, Space and Political Identities*, Malden, MA: Blackwell, 2008; p 63.

43 McNally, *Blood and Money*.

44 Ira Berlin and Philip Morgan, eds, *The Slaves' Economy*, Portland: Frank Cass, 1991; p 3.

45 Berlin and Morgan, *The Slaves' Economy*; p 8. Kamugisha, *Beyond Coloniality*.

46 James, *The Black Jacobins*.

## Chapter 4

1 Andreas Osiander, 'Sovereignty, international relations, and the Westphalian myth', *International Organization*, 55 (2) 2001: 251–87.

2 Pierre Bourdieu, *On the State: Lectures at the Collège de France, 1989–1992*, Cambridge: Polity, 2014.

3 Quoted in Warren Magnusson, *Politics of Urbanism: Seeing like a City*, London: Routledge, 2013; p 115.

4 Magnusson, *Politics of Urbanism*; p 116.

5 Magnusson, *Politics of Urbanism*; p 117.

6 Denis Cosgrove, 'Carto-City', in Janet Abrams and Peter Hall, eds, *Else/Where: Mapping New Cartographies of Networks and Territories*, Minneapolis: University of Minnesota Press, 2006, pp 148–57; p 148.

7 Cosgrove, 'Carto-City'; p 148.

8   See Maggie McCormick, 'Carto-City revisited: unmapping urbanness', in Elizabeth M. Grierson, ed, *Transformations: Art and the City*, Bristol: Intellect, 2017; pp 37–49.
9   Magnusson, *Politics of Urbanism*; p 117.
10  Eric Cline, *1177 BC: The Year Civilisation Collapsed*, Princeton, NJ: Princeton University Press, 2015.
11  See Josephine Quinn, 'Your Own Ships did this!' *London Review of Books*, 38 (4), 18 February 2016.
12  James C. Scott, *Seeing Like a State*, New Haven, CT: Yale University Press, 1998.
13  John Pickles, 'Text, hermeneutics and propaganda maps'; p 194.
14  Magnusson, *Politics of Urbanism*.
15  Magnusson, *Politics of* Urbanism; p 120.
16  Toscano, Alberto, and Jeff Kinkle,. *Cartographies of the Absolute*;. John Hunt Publishing, 2015. pp 15–16.
17  Piro Rexhepi, 'Unmapping Islam in Eastern Europe: periodisation and Muslim subjectivities in the Balkans', in Irene Kacandes and Yuliya Komska, eds, *Eastern Europe Unmapped: Beyond Borders and Peripheries*, New York: Berghahn Books, 2017, pp 53–4.
18  Rexhepi, 'Unmapping Islam in Eastern Europe'; pp 60–1.
19  Walter Benjamin, 'The Task of the Translator', *Illuminations*, trans. Harry Zohn; ed. and intro. Hannah Arendt, New York: Harcourt Brace Jovanovich, 1968, pp 69–82.
20  Benjamin, *Illuminations*; p 71.
21  Peter G. Mandaville, *Transnational Muslim Politics: Reimagining the Umma*, London: Routledge, 2003; p 70.
22  Ernst H. Kantorowicz, *The King's Two Bodies*, Princeton, NJ: Princeton University Press, 2016; Ernst H. Kantorowicz, 'Pro patria mori in Medieval Political Thought', *The American Historical Review* 56 (3) 1951: 472–92.
23  Sayyid Quṭb, *Milestones*, No. 512, Delhi: International Islamic Publishers, 1981.
24  Mandaville, *Transnational Muslim Politics*; p 70.
25  Peter Mandaville, *Global Political Islam*, London: Routledge, 2010.
26  Alison Pargeter, *The Muslim Brotherhood: From Opposition to Power*, London: Saqi, 2013.
27  Alison Pargeter, *Return to the Shadows: The Muslim Brotherhood and An-Nahda Since the Arab Spring*, London: Saqi, 2016.
28  Pargeter, *The Muslim Brotherhood*.
29  Carrie Rosefsky Wickham, *The Muslim Brotherhood: Evolution of an Islamist Movement*, Princeton, NJ: Princeton University Press, 2015.
30  Wickham, *The Muslim Brotherhood*.
31  Wickham, *The Muslim Brotherhood*.
32  Wickham, *The Muslim Brotherhood*.
33  Wickham, *The Muslim Brotherhood*.
34  Faisal Devji, *Landscapes of the Jihad: Militancy, Morality, Modernity*, Cornell University Press, 2005; p xvi.
35  Gilles Kepel and Pascale Ghazaleh, *The War for Muslim Minds: Islam and the West*, Cambridge, MA: Belknap Press of Harvard University Press, 2004.
36  Antoine Bousquet, 'Complexity theory and the war on terror: understanding the self-organising dynamics of leaderless jihad', *Journal of International Relations and* Development, 15 (3) 2012: 345–69.
37  Kepel and Ghazaleh, *The War for Muslim Minds*; p 141.
38  Jason Burke, *Al-Qaeda: The True Story of Radical Islam*, London: I. B. Tauris, 2004; p 261.
39  Marc Sageman, *Leaderless Jihad: Terror Networks in the Twenty-first Century*, Philadelphia: University of Pennsylvania Press, 2008; p 125. Daniel Kimmage and Kathleen Ridolfo, 'Iraq's networked insurgents', *Foreign Policy*, 163, 2007: 88–9. Kathleen Ridolfo

and Daniel Kimmage, *The War of Images and Ideas*, Washington, DC: Radio Free Europe/ Radio Liberty, 2007; p 17.

40 Kepel and Ghazaleh, *The War for Muslim Minds*; p 86. H. A. Hellyer, 'Ruminations and Reflections on British Muslims and Islam Post-7/7', in Tahir Abbas (ed.) *Islamic Political Radicalism: A European Perspective*, Edinburgh: Edinburgh University Press, 2007; p 247. Fawaz A. Gerges, *The Far Enemy: Why Jihad Went Global*, Cambridge: Cambridge University Press, 2005; p 151, p 191.

41 Gerges; p 151.

42 Hellyer, cited in Abbas; p 247.

43 Devji, *Landscapes of the Jihad*.

44 Burke, *Al-Qaeda*; p 275.

45 Paul Baines, Nicholas J. O'Shaughnessy, Kevin Moloney, Barry Richards, Sara Butler, and Mark Gill, *Muslim Voices: The British Muslim Response to Islamic Video Polemic – An Exploratory Study*, Research Paper 3/06, Bedford: Cranfield University School of Management, 2006.

46 Baines et al, *Muslim Voices*; p 81.

47 Sageman, *Leaderless Jihad*; p 144.

48 Devji, *Landscapes of the Jihad*.

49 Michel De Certeau, *The Practice of Everyday Life*, translated by Steven Rendall, Berkeley: University of California Press, 1988; p 129. Quoted in Sankaran Krishna, 'Cartographic anxiety: mapping the body politic in India', *Alternatives*, 19 (4) 1994: 507–21; p 203.

50 Devji, *Landscapes of the Jihad*.

51 Chandler, *Ontopolitics in the Anthropocene*.

# Chapter 5

1 Albert-Laszlo Barabasi, *Linked*, New York: Plume, 2003; p 4.

2 Mark Granovetter, 'The strength of weak ties', *American Journal of Sociology*, 78 (6) 1973: 1360–80; p 1378.

3 Francis Fukuyama, *The Origins of Political Order*, London: Profile, 2011; p 114.

4 Fukuyama, *The Origins of Political Order*; pp 113–14.

5 Peter Frankopan, *The Silk Roads*, London: Bloomsbury, 2015; p 15.

6 Frankopan, *The Silk Roads*; p 15.

7 Frankopan, *The Silk Roads*; p 23.

8 David Graeber, *The Utopia of Rules: On Technology, Stupidity, and the Secret Joys of Bureaucracy*, Brooklyn: Melville House, 2015; p 12.

9 Taken from Stewart Clegg, 'The end of bureaucracy?', in Thomas Diefenbach and Rune Todnem, eds, *Reinventing Hierarchy and Bureaucracy – from the Bureau to Network Organisations*, Bingley: Emerald Group Publishing, 2012, pp 59–84; p 65.

| Peters | Mao |
| --- | --- |
| Action-active decision-making | Permanent revolution |
| Close to the customer | Learn from the masses |
| Autonomy and entrepreneurship | Champion workers |
| Productivity through people | Learn from the masses |
| Hands-on, value-driven management | Mao's thinking driven by Red Guards/masses |

(continued)

| Peters | Mao |
|--------|-----|
| Stick to the knitting (what you know) | Communal principles as basis of organization |
| Simple form, lean staff | Mao's 20 lessons on bureaucracy (*Little Red Book*) |
| Simultaneous lean-tight properties | Mao's thinking as central and autonomy of local |
| (Shop floor autonomy/centralized values) | Communal-level Red Guards |

[10] Stuart Schram, ed, *Mao's Road to Power: Revolutionary Writings*, Vol II, Armonk, NY: East Gate Books, 1995; p 303.

[11] Peter Zarrow, *China in War and Revolution 1895–1949*, London: Routledge, 2005; p 96.

[12] Edgar Snow, *Red Star Over China*, New York: Grove Press, 1968; p 246. 'For hundreds of miles around there was only semipastoral country, the people lived in cave houses exactly as their ancestors did millenniums ago, many of the farmers still wore queues braided around their heads and the horse, the ass, and the camel were the latest thing in communications. Rape oil was used for lighting here, candles were a luxury, electricity was unknown, and foreigners were as rare as Eskimos in Africa. In this medieval world, it was astonishing to come upon soviet factories, and find machines turning, and a colony of workers busily producing the goods and tools of a Red China.'

[13] Snow, *Red Star Over China*; p 165.

[14] Lester Faigley, *Fragments of Rationality: Postmodernity and the Subject of Composition*, Pittsburgh: Pittsburgh University Press, 1992; p 10.

[15] Vladimir Lenin, *What Is to Be Done? Burning Questions of Our Movement*, Moscow: Foreign Languages Publishing House, 1950; p 149. Vladimir Lenin, *The State and Revolution*, London: Penguin, 1992.

[16] Reinhart Koselleck, *Critique and Crisis: Enlightenment and the Pathogenesis of Modern Society*, Cambridge, MA: MIT Press, 1988.

[17] Rosa Luxemburg, *The Mass Strike, The Political Party and the Trade Unions*, Colombo: Young Socialist Publications, 1964; p 17.

[18] Luxemburg, *The Mass Strike*; p 37.

[19] The Library of Congress, 37th Congress, 2nd Session, 1862, 'A Century of Lawmaking for a New Nation', http://memory.loc.gov/cgi-bin/ampage?collId=llsl&fileName=012/llsl012.db&recNum=522, accessed 5 November 2015.

[20] James Beniger, *The Control Revolution*, Cambridge, MA: Harvard University Press, 1986; pp 222–4.

[21] Beniger, *The Control Revolution*; p 224.

[22] Cameron Blevins, *Paper Trails: The US Post and the Making of the American West*, New York: Oxford University Press, 2021; p 4.

[23] Fritjof Capra, *The Hidden Connections*, London: Flamingo, 2003; p 133.

[24] Stanley McChrystal, *Team of Teams: New Rules of Engagement for a Complex World*, New York: Portfolio/Penguin, 2015; p 20.

[25] McChrystal, *Team of Teams*; pp 83–4.

[26] Stanley McChrystal, *My Share of the Task: A Memoir*, New York: Portfolio/Penguin, 2013; p 154.

[27] Fred Kaplan, *The Insurgents*, New York: Simon & Schuster, 2013; p 214.

[28] McChrystal, *My Share of the Task*; p 154.

[29] Robert Gates, Landon Lecture Series on Public Issues, 27 November 2007.

[30] Charlie Winter, lecture, King's College London, 15 November 2021.

# Chapter 6

1 Gilles Deleuze and Félix Guattari, *A Thousand Plateaus: Capitalism and Schizophrenia*, London: Bloomsbury Publishing, 1988.

2 Antoine Bousquet, *The Scientific Way of Warfare: Order and Chaos on the Battlefields of Modernity*, New York: Columbia University Press, 2009.

3 John Arquilla and David Ronfeldt, *Swarming and the Future of Conflict*, Santa Monica, CA: Rand, 2000.

4 Arquilla and Ronfeldt, *Swarming and the Future of Conflict*; p vii.

5 Arquilla and Ronfeldt, *Swarming and the Future of Conflict*; p viii.

6 Arquilla and Ronfeldt, *Swarming and the Future of Conflict*; p 5.

7 For an excellent discussion of the history of the 'martial gaze', see Antoine Bousquet, *The Eye of War: Military Perception from the Telescope to the Drone*, Minneapolis: University of Minnesota Press, 2018.

8 Arquilla and Ronfeldt, *Swarming and the Future of Conflict*.

9 Arquilla and Ronfeldt, *Swarming and the Future of Conflict*; p 20.

10 William E. Connolly, *Facing the Planetary: Entangled Humanism and the Politics of Swarming*, Durham, NC: Duke University Press, 2017.

11 Rosa Luxemburg, *The Mass Strike, the Political Party and the Trade Unions*, Detroit: Marxian Education Society, 1985.

12 Hannah Arendt, *On Revolution*, London: Penguin, 2006.

13 Alexander R. Galloway, *Protocol: How Control Exists after Decentralization*, Cambridge, MA: MIT Press, 2004.

14 Arquilla and Ronfeldt, *Swarming and the Future of Conflict*; p 67.

15 Paul Virilio and Sylvere Lotringer, *Pure War*, translated by Mark Polizzotti and Brian O'Keefe, New York: Semiotext(e), 1997.

16 David Chandler, *Ontopolitics in the Anthropocene*, London: Routledge, 2018; p 78.

17 Jeremy Walker and Melinda Cooper, 'Genealogies of resilience: from systems ecology to the political economy of crisis adaptation', *Security Dialogue*, 42 (2) 2011: 143–60.

18 Connolly, *Facing the Planetary*.

19 Connolly, *Facing the Planetary*; p 172.

20 Claudia Aradau and Rens Van Munster, *Politics of Catastrophe: Genealogies of the Unknown*, London: Routledge, 2011.

21 Galloway, *Protocol*; p 905.

22 Tudorel Vilcan, 'Articulating resilience in practice: chains of responsibilisation, failure points and political contestation', *Resilience*, 5 (1) 2017: 29–43.

23 Tsing, *The Mushroom at the End of the World*.

24 Walker and Cooper, 'Genealogies of resilience'.

25 Tsing, *The Mushroom at the End of the World*.

26 David Chandler and Julian Reid, *The Neoliberal Subject: Resilience, Adaptation and Vulnerability*, London: Rowman & Littlefield, 2016.

27 Chandler and Reid, *The Neoliberal Subject*.

28 Jürgen Habermas, *The Postnational Constellation: Political Essays*, New York: John Wiley & Sons, 2018.

29 Claudia Aradau and Rens Van Munster, 'Governing terrorism through risk: taking precautions, (un) knowing the future', *European Journal of International Relations*, 13 (1) 2007: 89–115.

30 Bratton, Boyadjiev, and Axel, *The New Normal*.

31 Régis Debray, *Revolution in the Revolution? Armed Struggle and Political Struggle in Latin America*, Harmondsworth: Penguin, 1968.

32 Debray, *Revolution in the Revolution?* p 24.

33 Debray, *Revolution in the Revolution?* p 24.

34  Ernesto Guevara, *Guerrilla Warfare*, BN Publishing, 2007.
35  Guevara, *Guerrilla Warfare*.
36  Guevara, *Guerrilla Warfare*; p 11.
37  Guevara, *Guerrilla Warfare*.
38  Guevara, *Guerrilla Warfare*; p 17.
39  Guevara, *Guerrilla Warfare*; p 13.
40  Debray, *Revolution in the Revolution*; p 48.
41  Debray, *Revolution in the Revolution*; p 54.
42  Guevara, *Guerrilla Warfare*; p 13.
43  Guevara, *Guerrilla Warfare*; p 14.
44  Guevara, *Guerrilla Warfare*; p 14.
45  Guevara, *Guerrilla Warfare*; p 82.
46  Guevara, *Guerrilla Warfare*; p 34.
47  Debray, *Revolution in the Revolution?* p 8.
48  Nicholas Michelsen and Pablo de Orellana, 'Pessimism and the alt-right: knowledge, power, race and time', in Tim Stevens and Nicholas Michelsen, eds, *Pessimism in International Relations*, Cham: Palgrave Macmillan, 2020, pp 119–36.

## Chapter 7

1  Keith Sugden, 'A history of the abacus', *The Accounting Historians Journal*, 8 (2) 1981: 1–22; p 2.
2  Massimo Sargiacomo, Stefano Coronella, Chiara Mio, Ugo Sostero, and Roberto Di Petra, eds, *The Origins of Accounting Culture: The Venetian Connection*, New York: Routledge, 2018; p 2.
3  Alan Sangster, Gregory N. Stoner, and Patricia A. McCarthy, 'The market for Luca Pacioli's *Summa Arithmetica*', *The Accounting Historians Journal*, 35 (1) 2008: 111–35; pp 115–6.
4  Sargiacomo et al, *The Origins of Accounting Culture*; pp 3–4.
5  Riccardo Mori, 'The machine that changed the world – transcription of the interview with Steve Jobs', 5 March 2020, https://morrick.me/archives/8816, accessed 29 July 2021.
6  Dan Bricklin, 'Meet the inventor of the electronic spreadsheet', TED Talk, https://www.ted.com/talks/dan_bricklin_meet_the_inventor_of_the_electronic_spreadsheet, accessed 29 July 2021.
7  Michael Power, 'The audit society', in Anthony Hopwood and Peter Miller, eds, *Accounting as Social and Institutional Practice*, Cambridge: Cambridge University Press, 1994, pp 299–316; p 309.
8  Benedict Anderson, *Imagined Communities: Reflections on the Origin and Spread of Nationalism*, London: Verso Books, 2006.
9  Hobbes, *Leviathan*; Part 1, Chapter 4, pp 100–1.
10  Sharon Achinstein, *Milton and the Revolutionary Reader*, Princeton, NJ: Princeton University Press, 1994; p 85.
11  James Holstun, *Pamphlet Wars: Prose in the English Revolution*, London: Frank Cass, 1992; p 24.
12  Michel Foucault, *Discipline and Punish: The Birth of the Prison*, London: Penguin, 1975.
13  BBC News, 'Facebook warns growth set to slow "significantly"', 28 July 2021, https://www.bbc.co.uk/news/business-58006689, accessed 29 July 2021. Omnicore, 'Instagram by the numbers: stats, demographics & fun facts', https://www.omnicoreagency.com/instagram-statistics/, accessed 4 January 2022.
14  Lefebvre, 'Space and the state'; p 85.

15  Elias Canetti, *Crowds and Power*, New York: Farrar, Straus and Giroux, 1984.

16  Paul Virilio and Sylvère Lotringer, *Pure War*, Los Angeles: Semiotext(e), 2008 [1983].

17  Peter F. Drucker, *The Age of Discontinuity: Guidelines to Our Changing Society*, London: Heinemann, 1970; p 10 (emphasis added).

18  Manuel Castells, *The Rise of the Network Society*, Malden, MA: Blackwell, 2000.

19  Ankie Hoogvelt, *Globalisation and the Postcolonial World*, Baltimore: John Hopkins University Press, 1997.

20  Arjun Appadurai, 'Disjuncture and difference in the global cultural economy', *Theory, Culture & Society*, 7 (2–3) 1990: 295–310; pp 296–7.

21  Appadurai, 'Disjuncture and difference in the global cultural economy'; p 295.

22  Carney, cited in Nelly Stromquist and Karen Monkman, *Globalisation and Education: Integration and Contestation Across Cultures*, Lanham, MD: Rowman & Littlefield Education, 2014; p 122.

23  Anthony Giddens, *The Nation-State and Violence*, Cambridge: Polity Press, 1985; p 33.

24  Ulrich Beck, *Risk Society: Towards a New Modernity*, London: SAGE, 1992.

25  Steven Vogel, *Freer Markets, More Rules*, Ithaca: Cornell University Press, 1998; p 3.

26  Mariana Mazuccato, *The Entrepreneurial State*, London: Anthem Press, 2013; pp 101–2.

27  Philip Bobbitt, *Terror and Consent*, London: Allen Lane, 2008; p 88.

28  Stewart Brand, 'We owe it all to the hippies', *Time*, 1 March 1995, http://content.time.com/time/subscriber/article/0,33009,982602,00.html, accessed 3 December 2015.

29  Fred Turner, *From Counterculture to Cyberculture*, Chicago: University of Chicago Press, 2006; p 103.

30  Walter Isaacson, *The Innovators: How a Group of Hackers, Geniuses and Geeks Created the Digital Revolution*, New York: Simon & Schuster, 2014; p 271.

31  World Wide Web Foundation, 'History of the web', http://webfoundation.org/about/vision/history-of-the-web/, accessed 3 December 2015.

32  'The creed of speed', *The Economist*, 5 December 2015, p 23.

33  Mazuccato, *The Entrepreneurial State*; pp 101–2.

34  Mazuccato, *The Entrepreneurial State*; p 102.

35  Mazuccato, *The Entrepreneurial State*; pp 105–6.

36  Anatole Kaletsky, *Capitalism 4.0*, London: Bloomsbury, 2011; p 2.

37  Hyde, *Common as Air*; pp 190–1.

38  Berry and Galloway, 'A Network is a Network is a Network'.

39  Alexander Galloway, *Protocol, or, How Control Exists after Decentralisation*, Cambridge, MA: MIT Press, 2004.

40  Galloway, *Protocol*; loc 486.

41  McKenzie Wark, *A Hacker Manifesto*, Cambridge, MA: Harvard University Press, 2004.

42  Galloway, *Protocol*.

43  Galloway, *Protocol*; see also Roger Griffin, 'From slime mould to rhizome: an introduction to the groupuscular right', *Patterns of Prejudice*, 37 (1) 2003: 27–50.

44  David Golombia, *The Politics of Bitcoin*, Minneapolis: University of Minnesota Press, 2016.

45  Peter A. Thiel and Blake Masters, *Zero to One: Notes on Startups, or How to Build the Future*, New York: Crown Business, 2014. Jonathan Taplin, *Move Fast and Break Things: How Facebook, Google, and Amazon Cornered Culture and Undermined Democracy*, New York: Little, Brown, 2017.

46  David Chandler, *Ontopolitics in the Anthropocene*. See also this point in Bryant, *Onto-cartography*.

47  Bryant, *Onto-cartography*.

48  Galloway, *Protocol*.

[49] Branden Hookway, *Pandemonium: The Rise of Predatory Locales in the Postwar World*, New York: Princeton Architectural Press, 1999; p 81.

## Chapter 8

[1] Culp, *Dark Deleuze*; p 7.

[2] Culp, *Dark Deleuze*; p 16.

[3] Janet Abrams and Peter Hall, eds, *Else/Where: Mapping New Cartographies of Networks and Territories*, Minneapolis: University of Minnesota Press, 2006; p 14.

[4] Abrams and Hall, *Else/Where*; p 12.

[5] Abrams and Hall, *Else/Where*; p 192.

[6] Armand Mattelart, 'Mapping modernity: utopia and communication networks', in Denis Cosgrove, ed, *Mappings*, London: Reaktion Books, 1999; pp 169–92; p 176.

[7] Todd Wolfson, *Digital Rebellion: The Birth of the Cyber Left*, Urbana, IL: University of Illinois Press, 2014; p 16.

[8] Jeffrey S. Juris, 'Anarchism, or the cultural logic of networking', in Randall Amster, Abraham DeLeon, Luis Fernandez, Anthony J. Nocella II, and Deric Shannon, eds, *Contemporary Anarchist Studies: An Introductory Anthology of Anarchy in the Academy*, London: Routledge, 2009, pp 213–23.

[9] David Graeber, 'For a new anarchism', *New Left Review*, 13, 2002: 61.

[10] Connolly, *Facing the Planetary*, p 75.

[11] Sam Halvorsen, 'Beyond the network? Occupy London and the global movement', *Social Movement Studies* 11 (3–4) 2012: 427–33.

[12] Paolo Gerbaudo, 'The persistence of collectivity in digital protest', *Information, Communication & Society*, 17 (2) 2014: 264–8. See also Paolo Gerbaudo, 'Social media teams as digital vanguards: the question of leadership in the management of key Facebook and Twitter accounts of Occupy Wall Street, Indignados and UK Uncut', *Information, Communication & Society*, 20 (2) 2017: 185–202.

[13] Paolo Gerbaudo, 'The persistence of collectivity in digital protest'; p 267.

[14] Wolfson, *Digital Rebellion*; p 21.

[15] Dick Van Weelden, 'Possible worlds', in Janet Abrams and Peter Hall, eds, *Else/Where: Mapping New Cartographies of Networks and Territories*, Minneapolis: University of Minnesota Press, 2006; pp 26–9.

[16] Galloway, *Protocol*.

[17] Nick Srnicek and Alex Williams, *Inventing the Future: Postcapitalism and a World without Work*, London: Verso, 2016.

[18] Connolly, *Facing the Planetary*; pp 144–5.

[19] Connolly, *Facing the Planetary*.

[20] Culp, *Dark Deleuze*; p 46.

[21] Louise Beam, 'Leaderess resistence', *The Seditionist*, 12, 1992, www.louisbeam.com/leaderless.htm, accessed 11 February 2022.

[22] Beam, 'Leaderess resistence'.

[23] Culp, *Dark Deleuze*; p 49.

[24] Culp, *Dark Deleuze*.

[25] Galloway, *Protocol*.

[26] Mark Fisher, *Ghosts of My Life: Writings on Depression, Hautology and Lost Futures*, Winchester: Zero Books, 2014.

[27] Frederick Jameson, *The Cultural Logic of Late Capitalism*. See Brian Holmes, 'Counter cartographies', in Janet Abrams and Peter Hall, eds, *Else/Where: Mapping New*

*Cartographies of Networks and Territories*, Minneapolis: University of Minnesota Press, 2006; pp 20–25, p 20.

28  Toscano and Kinkle, *Cartographies of the Absolute*; p 69.

29  Griffin, 'From slime mould to rhizome'.

30  Angela Nagle, *Kill all Normies: Online Culture Wars from 4chan and Tumblr to Trump and the Alt-right*, Charlotte, NC: John Hunt Publishing, 2017.

31  Nagle, *Kill all Normies*; p 13.

32  Nicholas Michelsen and Pablo De Orellana, 'Discourses of resilience in the US alt-right', *Resilience* 7 (3) 2019: 271–87. Elisabeth Sandifer, *Neoreaction a Basilisk: Essays on and around the Alt-right*, Eruditorum Press, 2017. Joshua Tait, 'Mencius Moldbug and neoreaction', in Mark Sedgewick, ed, *Key Thinkers of the Radical Right: Behind the New Threat to Liberal Democracy*, New York: Oxford University Press, 2019, pp 187–203.

33  Nagle, *Kill all Normies*.

34  The Invisible Committee, *The Coming Insurrection*, Cambridge, MA: MIT Press, 2008.

35  The Invisible Committee, *The Coming Insurrection*; p 60.

36  The Invisible Committee, *The Coming Insurrection*; pp 111–12.

37  The Invisible Committee, *The Coming Insurrection*; p 61, p 124.

38  The Invisible Committee, *The Coming Insurrection*; p 108.

39  The Invisible Committee, *The Coming Insurrection*; pp 113–14.

40  Carlos Marighella, *For the Liberation of Brazil*, Harmondsworth: Penguin Books, 1971; p 32.

41  Marighella, *For the Liberation of Brazil*; p 47.

42  Marighella, *For the Liberation of Brazil*; p 57–8.

43  Marighella, *For the Liberation of Brazil*; p 57.

44  Neville Bolt, *The Violent Image: Insurgent Propaganda and the New Revolutionaries*, New York: Columbia University Press, 2011, 2021.

45  Neville Bolt, 'Propaganda of the deed and its anarchist origins', in Paul Baines, Nicholas O'Shaughnessy, and Nancy Snow, eds, *The SAGE Handbook of Propaganda*, London: SAGE, 2021.

46  Michael Bakunin, *Statism and Anarchy*, translated and edited by Marshall S. Shatz, Cambridge: Cambridge University Press, 1990.

47  Nicholas Michelsen, 'Horizontalism is a map', in Pol Bargués-Pedreny, David Chandler, and Elena Simon, eds, *Mapping and Politics in the Digital Age*, London: Routledge, 2019, pp 56–71; p 60.

48  Sergeï Gennadievich Nechayev, *The Catechism of the Revolutionist*, London: Kropotkin's Lighthouse Publications, 1971.

49  Nicholas Kiersey and Wanda Vrasti, 'A convergent genealogy? Space, time and the promise of horizontal politics today', *Capital & Class* 40 (1) 2016: 75–94; p 84.

50  Wolfson, *Digital Rebellion*.

51  Kiersey and Vrasti, 'A convergent genealogy?'

52  Erica Lagalisse, 2019, *Occult Features of Anarchism: With Attention to the Conspiracy of Kings and the Conspiracy of the Peoples*, Oakland, CA: PM Press; p 20.

53  Lagalisse, *Occult Features of Anarchism*.

54  Kiersey and Vrasti, 'A convergent genealogy?'; p 6.

55  Kiersey and Vrasti, 'A convergent genealogy?'

56  Todd Wolfson, *Digital Rebellion: The Birth of the Cyber Left*, Urbana, Chicago, and Springfield, IL: University of Illinois Press, 2014, p 44.

57  Michelsen, 'Horizontalism is a map'; p 61.

58  Connolly, *Facing the Planetary*; p 121.
59  Connolly, *Facing the Planetary*; p 128.
60  Connolly, *Facing the Planetary*; p 35.
61  World Economic Forum, *Global Risk Report*, 14th Edition, 2019, https://www3.wefo rum.org/docs/WEF_Global_Risks_Report_2019.pdf, accessed 11 February 2022.
62  Thomas Knutson et al, 'Tropical cyclones and climate change assessment: Part II: Projected response to anthropogenic warming', *Bulletin of the American Meteorological Society*, 101 (3) 2020: E303–E322.
63  Savin S. Chand et al, 'Projected increase in El Niño-driven tropical cyclone frequency in the Pacific', *Nature Climate Change*, 7 (2) 2017: 123–7. Hiroyuki Murakami et al, 'Future changes in tropical cyclone activity projected by the new high-resolution MRI-AGCM', *Journal of Climate* 25 (9) 2012: 3237–60.
64  Malcolm John Roberts et al, 'Projected future changes in tropical cyclones using the CMIP6 HighResMIP multimodel ensemble', *Geophysical Research Letters*, 47 (14) 2020: e2020GL088662.
65  Timothy Morton, *Hyperobjects: Philosophy and Ecology after the End of the World*, Minneapolis: University of Minnesota Press, 2013; Introduction.
66  Tsing, *The Mushroom at the End of the World*.
67  Anatol Lieven, *Climate Change and the Nation State: The Case for Nationalism in a Warming World*, New York: Oxford University Press, 2020.
68  Didier Bigo, 'Globalised (in)security: the field and the ban-opticon', in Didier Bigo and Anastassia Tsoukala, eds, *Terror, Insecurity and Liberty: Illiberal Practices of Liberal Regimes After 9/11*, London: Routledge, 2008, pp 10–48; p 18.
69  Anne-Marie Slaughter, *A New World*, Princeton, NJ: Princeton University Press, 2004; p 5.
70  Lieven, *Climate Change and the Nation State*.
71  Pablo De Orellana and Nicholas Michelsen. 'Reactionary internationalism: the philosophy of the new right', *Review of International Studies* 45 (5) 2019: 748–67.

## Chapter 9

1  Peter Frankopan, *The Silk Roads*, London: Bloomsbury, 2015; pp 46–7.
2  Frankopan, *The Silk Roads*; pp 46–7.
3  Nicola Smith, 'Turkey will shoot to kill as it builds wall on border with ISIS', *The Sunday Times*, World News, 13 December 2015, p 30.
4  Joel Migdal, *Mental Maps and Virtual Checkpoints in Boundaries and Belonging: States and Societies in the Struggle to Shape Identities and Local Practices*, Cambridge: Cambridge University Press, 2004; p 11.
5  Maxim Bolt, *Zimbabwe's Migrants and South Africa's Border Farms: The Roots of Impermanence*, New York: Cambridge University Press, 2015.
6  Bolt, *Zimbabwe's Migrants and South Africa's Border Farms*; p 4.
7  Bolt, *Zimbabwe's Migrants and South Africa's Border Farms*.
8  Janet Roitman, 'Power is not sovereign: the pluralisation of economic regulatory authority in the Chad Basin', in Beatrice Hibou, ed, *Privatising the State*, London: Hurst, 2004, pp 120–46; pp 121–2.
9  Judith Scheele, *Smugglers and Saints of the Sahara: Regional Connectivity in the Twentieth Century*, Cambridge: Cambridge University Press, 2012; p 3.
10  Scheele, *Smugglers and Saints of the Sahara*; p 4. See also maps of trade networks in Ghislaine Lydon, *On Trans-Saharan Trails*, New York: Cambridge University Press, 2009; pp xxiii–xxviii.
11  Scheele, *Smugglers and Saints of the Sahara*; p 6.

[12] Lydon, *On Trans-Saharan Trails*; pp xxiii–xxviii.

[13] Scheele, *Smugglers and Saints of the Sahara*; p 14.

[14] Roitman, 'Power is not sovereign'; p 121.

[15] Roitman, 'Power is not sovereign'; pp 135–6.

[16] Alison Pargeter, *Libya: The Rise and Fall of Qaddafi*, New Haven, CT: Yale University Press, 2012; p 15.

[17] See Yvan Guichaoua, 'Tuareg militancy and the Sahelian shockwaves of the Libyan revolution', in Peter Cole and Brian McQuinn, eds, *The Libyan Revolution and its Aftermath*, Oxford: Oxford University Press, 2015.

[18] Stephen Harmon, *Terror and Insurgency*, Farnham: Ashgate, 2014; p 179.

[19] Guichaoua, 'Tuareg militancy'.

[20] Cited in Max Hastings, 'The curse of 1916', *The Sunday Times*, News Review, 3 January 2016.

[21] Hastings, 'The curse of 1916'.

[22] Alessandro Scafi, 'Mapping Eden' in Denis Cosgrove, ed, *Mappings*, London: Reaktion Books, 1999; pp 42–72, p 53.

[23] Scafi, 'Mapping Eden'; p 64.

[24] Scafi, 'Mapping Eden'; p 66.

[25] Cited in Laura Kurgan, *Close Up at a Distance: Mapping, Technology, and Politics*, Cambridge, MA: MIT Press, 2013; p 9. Abrams and Hall, *Else/Where*.

[26] Toscano and Kinkle, *Cartographies of the Absolute*; p 24.

[27] L. R. Bryant, *Onto-cartography: An Ontology of Machines and Media*, Edinburgh: Edinburgh University Press, 2014; p 124.

## Conclusion

[1] Koselleck, *Critique and Crisis*.

[2] Sharman, *Empires of the Weak*; p 66.

## Afterword

[1] Deleuze and Guattari, *A Thousand Plateaus*. See also Deleuze and Guattari, *Anti-Oedipus*. The secondary literature is expansive, but a reader might set out with the following texts: Brian Massumi, *A User's Guide to Capitalism and Schizophrenia: Deviations from Deleuze and Guattari*, Cambridge, MA: MIT Press, 1992; Jay Lampert, *Deleuze and Guattari's Philosophy of History*, London: Continuum, 2006; Gregg Lambert, *Who's Afraid of Deleuze and Guattari?* London: Continuum, 2006; Eleanor Kaufman and Kevin Jon Heller, eds, *Deleuze and Guattari: New Mappings in Politics, Philosophy, and Culture*, Minneapolis: University of Minnesota Press, 1998; De Landa, *A Thousand Years of Nonlinear History*; De Landa, *Intensive Science and Virtual Philosophy*; Ian Buchanan, ed, *A Deleuzian Century?* Durham, NC: Duke University Press, 1999; Nicholas Michelsen, *Politics and Suicide: The Philosophy of Political Self-destruction*, London: Routledge, 2015.

# Index